# THE HISPANIC CHALLENGE

## *Opportunities* Confronting the Church

# Manuel Ortiz

INTERVARSITY PRESS
DOWNERS GROVE, ILLINOIS 60515

*To my courageous parents,*
*Manuel and Luisa,*
*who came to this country*
*with a concern for their future and family*
*and discovered*
*the riches of Christ.*
*This truth they shared with me.*

*InterVarsity Press® is the book-publishing division of InterVarsity Christian Fellowship®, a student movement active on campus at hundreds of universities, colleges and schools of nursing in the United States of America, and a member movement of the International Fellowship of Evangelical Students. For information about local and regional activities, write Public Relations Dept., InterVarsity Christian Fellowship, 6400 Schroeder Rd., P.O. Box 7895, Madison, WI 53707-7895.*

*All Scripture quotations, unless otherwise indicated, are taken from the HOLY BIBLE, NEW INTERNATIONAL VERSION®. NIV®. Copyright ©1973, 1978, 1984 by International Bible Society. Used by permission of Zondervan Publishing House. All rights reserved.*

*ISBN 0-8308-1773-5*

*Printed in the United States of America*

**Library of Congress Cataloging-in-Publication Data**

*Ortiz, Manuel, 1938-*
   *The Hispanic challenge: opportunities confronting the church/*
*Manuel Ortiz.*
    *p.  cm.*
   *Includes bibliographical references.*
    *ISBN 0-8308-1773-5 (alk. paper)*
    *1. Church work with Hispanic Americans.    2. Hispanic Americans—*
*Religion.   I.  Title.*
   *BV4468.2.H57077    1993*
*261.8'34868073—dc20*
                                                              *93-41900*
                                                                      *CIP*

| 19 | 18 | 17 | 16 | 15 | 14 | 13 | 12 | 11 | 10 | 9 | 8 | 7 | 6 | 5 | 4 | 3 | 2 | 1 |
|----|----|----|----|----|----|----|----|----|----|----|----|----|----|----|----|----|----|----|
| 08 | 07 | 06 | 05 | 04 | 03 | 02 | 01 | 00 | 99 | 98 | 97 | 96 | 95 | 94 | 93 | | | |

## Foreword

Manuel (Manny) Ortiz was a name I began to hear almost immediately after moving to Illinois ten years ago, usually in the context of being informed that this was a man I "just had to meet." Several months later I did meet him, and found in him a wonderful brother in Christ.

We have much in common, Manny and I. We are both Hispanic. We both grew up in New York City during a period in which assimilation was the dominant theme in American society. The "melting pot" and Horatio Alger myths were still accepted as reality. The message was conveyed, directly and indirectly, sometimes subtly, sometimes blatantly, but always clearly: If you worked hard enough, you could be whoever and do whatever you wished. The key to success was always tied to the knowledge and use of English and becoming a "real American." Giving up Spanish in favor of English would have two positive outcomes. First, you would not be negatively stereotyped as Puerto Rican—important at a time when being a "Rican" was practically synonymous with being in gangs, thanks to *West Side Story* and the local media. Second, you would gain the most important tool for success in America.

What followed this formula for "success," however, was questions, the answers to which were potentially devastating. What did it mean when your parents played by the rules but did not attain the American symbols of success? What were the consequences when, after giving up the language of your birth, you discovered that you were also rejecting your culture, history and heritage? Who, or what, were you when you were no longer Puerto Rican but not accepted as Anglo?

Until I met Manny, these and similar questions were a part of my personal struggles that I thought were unique, a result of my own inadequacies. True, as a result of my training as a sociologist, sometime earlier I had begun to recognize that there were historical and sociological explanations for my struggles, but I had never been able to share them with a Latino brother. Manny understood. He shared my struggles, and we helped each other reframe the questions as *our* questions—the questions of a marginalized people. In addition, he opened up a new world where I found Christian brothers and sisters who struggled to make sense of what it meant to be Latino and Christian and to understand how one experience could inform the other.

In chapter three Manny recounts something of his biography and the biographies of other Hispanics. This may be the key to understanding the challenge of ministering to and evangelizing the second and third generations of Hispanics (and other immigrant groups). These experiences have contributed much to Manny's missiological wisdom. He doesn't stop with personal stories. He moves beyond them to principles of ministry based on biblical models. He presents models of ministry, raising related issues and identifying strengths and weaknesses. Manny has been a teacher and mentor to those who would minister, and he continues that role here.

Manny understands our struggle. He understands that there are dimensions unique to our people and others that we share in common with Christians everywhere. He understands, further, that the challenge of bringing the gospel of Jesus Christ to our Latino community is one for which we must accept responsibility. And, yet, he recognizes that we dare not leave out any within the body of believers. To do so would make us guilty of the same practices of exclusion and marginalization we have suffered.

In this book, as in his life and ministry, Manny models for us the servant's struggle to integrate spirituality and justice. He has been motivated by an understanding of the importance of the Great Commission. At the same time he recognizes this is not the only scriptural mandate. He knows and teaches that our attempts to evangelize will lack credibility if we fail "to do justice, to love mercy and to walk humbly with our God." This volume fills a number of needs in the evangelical community. It informs us about Hispanics in the United States, it identifies existing needs, and suggests approaches and strategies to meet them. For individuals, churches and organizations considering Hispanic ministry, *The Hispanic Challenge* is an excellent place to start. For those who have already begun, it provides an excellent resource and encouragement to continue.

*Alvaro L. Nieves*
*Wheaton College*

# Preface

This book expresses a journey of life that started with my first visit to the farms of New Jersey, where I saw my relatives working as cheap labor and living in shacks under horrible conditions, and continued to the streets of Spanish Harlem, where we learned that because we were Puerto Ricans we could not walk outside of our neighborhood for fear of violent attacks. I am thankful for the many who guided my path, including my godparents, who shared their resources and energy to see both their children and me succeed.

I am often stunned to see that life has not changed in any drastic way that would assure me that my children and their children will live in a better society. The analysis provided in this volume points to a future that will need many committed and devoted servants of the Lord who are willing to place their lives in the hands of the Lord and be led by the Spirit to share the good news in the inner city.

We are losing our Hispanic youth to gangs, drug addiction and systems of evil that ignore the educational development of our young people. We need churches that will not only stay in the city but will also provide programs that will be useful on the streets of our major urban communities. Who will be the models of grace and righteousness? How will we promote healthy families when our families that are growing in mercy and love are moving away from the most needy and ignored areas of our cities? This volume is intended to reach the hearts of Christians who truly believe that God is sovereign, even in the cities of our country, and who are willing to proclaim and live the healing gospel of Christ to all who will hear.

After five years of living in the Bartram Village projects of Philadelphia, where I served the Lord through my local church, Christian Union Church, and then fifteen years in Chicago, working with youth on the streets and developing leadership for new churches, I know that the only solution to humanity's dilemma and dehumanization is found in Christ our Lord. Although the beginning of this book may seem too sociological because of the analysis, look deeper and recognize that the analysis only provides us with a sign of where the shalom of God is missing.

In the early days of my conversion, Bill and Mary Krispin provided the necessary teaching that would eventually become the base of my doing ministry in the city. In the early stages of my work in Chicago, the Reverend Clarence Hilliard became a friend and mentor, and both he and his wife, Annie, have been examples of love for the poor and the oppressed.

I am deeply grateful to those who served with me in Chicago—Fernando Aviles, Pedro Aviles, Gaby Caballero, Juan Flores, Tony Gonzalez, Ray Maldonado, Johnny Matias, Olga Vasquez Pantoja and José Rivera—and especially to the elders/church planters of Spirit and Truth Fellowship—Randy and Sue Baker, Bob and Evelyn Crawford, and Esteban Lugo. This mission team provided my family with the resources so often missing in the city—love and encouragement. Mission in the city depends on both the calling of God and the community of faith. I certainly made numerous blunders, mistakes that were visible and public, but the support of God's people was always there, ready to forgive and go on with the task.

Now, as I find my ministry both in North Philadelphia and in

Westminster Theological Seminary as an associate professor of practical theology, my dear friend Dr. Harvie Conn and his wife, Dorothy, have assisted me in my growth and transition into the life of the seminary where students are being challenged with missions to the city and the poor. I am deeply indebted to Harvie's modeling.

As a second-generation Puerto Rican, I realize the enormous task my children have ahead of them. They have provided me with insights and joy when there was little to smile about. Thank you, Debbie and Hector, Joe and Martha, Elizabeth and José, and Stephen, for your faithful companionship. I especially want to thank Blanca, my companion in mission. My wife has been a true missionary who understands from the depth of her heart the Lord's concern for the poor.

This work needed ongoing revisions and reflection, and Sue Baker graciously made time to do what was needed. Thank you.

The time draws near for all of us to recognize the shortage of life left here on earth. May God grant us hearts that realize the joy of sharing the good news of Christ with a hurting and lost world.

*Manuel Ortiz*
*Philadelphia, Pennsylvania*

# Introduction

The Rodríguezes were torn between leaving their native Cuba, which had experienced strife first under the dictatorship of Batista and even more under Castro, and staying in the country they loved so deeply. When they decided to leave, they felt sad but also hopeful that in the U.S. they would experience what many had been saying—that it was the land of opportunity, the world's most generous country. They knew nothing could ever replace their motherland, but what choice did they have? They decided to join their family, who had already settled in Florida and boasted of a new life free of dictatorship and danger.

For some time Juan Lebrón had been unable to secure a steady job in Puerto Rico. He worked for construction companies on a day-to-day basis, but he could never count on a consistent paycheck to support his family. His cousin suggested a trip to New York City, where many of their relatives had been living since they first went to work on a New Jersey farm. Juan resisted at first. Why would he want to leave his country of warmth and friendliness for an unknown city devoid of trees, mountains, pleasant temperatures and many of his loved ones? But eventually, unemployment led Juan to accept his cousin's advice. He convinced his young wife that New York would be their big chance to begin a new life together and establish the large family they so desired. "I will never forget the mixed emotions of leaving," Juan remembers. "How fearful we felt when in the cold of January we landed in an overcrowded airport where most people were wearing coats and I was in my white long-sleeved shirt."

Jaime Villarreal can remember the stories his grandfather would tell of building railways in southern California, New Mexico and Nevada. His grandfather and the other Mexicans worked for extremely low wages, lower than all other immigrants. It was a sad story, yet Jaime felt excited as he heard about a country he had never seen and people that were different. He especially enjoyed the stories of his grandfather's work in Texas, where they harvested cotton and vegetables grown on irrigated land. Without these Mexican workers, his grandfather said, the Texans would never have succeeded in creating such profitable farms and ranches. Even though the low pay seemed unfair, Jaime wanted to make more of his life than what his town seemed to offer. He longed to try this new place, but he knew that moving to the U.S. would cause problems for him and his family. Sometimes he thought the real reason he wanted to leave Mexico was the helplessness he felt as he watched his parents live under poor and disadvantaged conditions.

The families described above have become part of the 22,354,059 Hispanics (not including recent and undocumented immigrants) counted in the 1990 census. The various Hispanic groups, when combined, have become the fastest growing minority group in the U.S.[1] Their influence on both the North American context and the Third World must be taken seriously in establishing mission strategy for the coming decade. As Orlando Costas has often said, the U.S. Hispanic community is a "sleeping giant."

These vignettes illustrate the varied experiences of those considered Hispanic in the U.S., those who have undergone the process of change in a new world. The children of these families have become part of the second generation, a group often excluded from histories or anthropological studies. I will focus on this group here not only because of my personal identification with it but also because of the missiological understanding that it is not being reached and incorporated into the church. I intend to provide a stimulus for Christians who have overlooked the second generation when considering the Hispanic community for ministry. Moreover, the second-generation phenomenon is not unique to the Hispanic population; it occurs in many other ethnic groups that have entered the U.S.

As a second-generation Puerto Rican born and raised in "el barrio" of New York City, I not only recognize the journeys described in these stories, but I also see an exciting future for U.S. churches that undertake the task of evangelism and leadership training among second-generation urban Hispanics.

This book is divided into three sections. The first addresses the question, Who are the Hispanics in the United States? It is a complex question and cannot be answered thoroughly in one volume. In order to gain a useful overview, I have chosen to focus on the three major Hispanic subgroups—Mexican, Puerto Rican and Cuban. I will examine demographics, historical information and ethnographic work in the form of narratives by second-generation Hispanics. This section serves as an introduction to some of the sociological and anthropological information that will assist pastors, missionaries and concerned Christians who desire to pray for and serve among urban Hispanics in the U.S.

The second section explores the various missiological issues we must consider in doing ministry among second-generation Hispanics. In presenting these issues, I will provide a theological foundation for the practical work of ministry within the Hispanic church. Justo González describes three basic errors in what is often called "narrative" theology. First, we unwittingly assume that the theology we learn in our universities and churches is "general" and nonethnic. Second, we think that "the interests of one minority will necessarily be opposed to the interests of another." And third, we believe that "a school of theology has more 'universal' significance when it avoids being tied down to a concrete historical and geographical setting."[2] In light of these prevailing attitudes, the theology I discuss in this section has a certain bias, but it arises out of my commitment to be faithful to the Scriptures and my ongoing reflection on the church's role specifically in the Hispanic community.

The final section will approach the subject of leadership and leadership training among second-generation Hispanics. Leadership is vital to the development of the Hispanic church. After providing a theological rationale, I cover both theoretical and practical issues of training leaders. Special attention is given to the practice of mentoring.

# SECTION I

---

# Hispanics
in the
United States:
A Sociohistoric
Overview

# Chapter 1

---

# Urbanization:
# The Hispanic
# Reality

Th
his chapter and the next two provide demographic, historical and ethnographic material that will help us to
understand the life experience of second-generation
Hispanics. As we shall see, their needs are oppressive and
demanding.

Let us begin by clarifying the meaning of *Hispanic*. Much discussion has taken place about what names to use to describe people
from Puerto Rico, Mexico, Central America, South America, Cuba
and those with Spanish surnames. That dialogue will probably
never lead to a definitive conclusion. As Isidro Lucas explains,

There are many names used to describe Latino communities.
Some correspond with national groupings—Puerto Rican, Chicano, or Mexican-American, etc. These names must be given
appropriate recognition, because they are reflections of each
individual's group attachment. In some parts of the country,

where a group has statistical prevalence, the term that corresponds to its national grouping is the one most often used.

In Chicago, where all major Latino groups are represented, more general terms are preferred, such as Latinos or Hispanics, although one must keep in mind that this lumping together of national groups into a "minority" is an artificial convenience.[1] On the larger sociological scale, for purposes of identity in statistical and political structures, *Latinos* and *Hispanics* have been the most prominent "markers." In the actual communities, however, people rarely use the terms *Hispanic* or *Latino* to describe themselves, except when discussing political matters. Instead, their description is based on ethnic identity: "I am Puerto Rican," "We are a Mexican-American community," and so on.

A recent national survey of Puerto Rican, Mexican and Cuban U.S. citizens and noncitizens[2] indicated an overwhelming preference for national-orgin labels as opposed to panethnic labels (Hispanic, Latino, etc.). Table 1.1 shows that Mexican and Cuban noncitizens have the strongest preference, with 87.7 percent and 88.5 percent respectively choosing their national origin, but even U.S. citizens (all Puerto Ricans are citizens) prefer the national-orgin label. It is also interesting to note the extremely low percentages that prefer being called "American," from 0.3 percent for Mexican noncitizens to 16.7 percent for Cuban citizens.

**Table 1.1:   Preferred Ethnic Label by Hispanic Subgroup and U.S. Citizenship, 1989-90**

| | Citizens | | | Noncitizens | |
|---|---|---|---|---|---|
| Preferred Label | Puerto Rican | Mexican | Cuban | Mexican | Cuban |
| National origin | 74.9% | 63.3% | 64.0% | 87.7% | 88.5% |
| Panethnic | 15.0% | 27.8% | 18.1% | 2.1% | 8.8% |
| "American" | 9.1% | 8.5% | 16.7% | 0.3% | 2.7% |
| Other | 1.0% | 0.3% | 1.2% | 0.0% | 0.0% |

Source: "Datanote on the Puerto Rican Community," *Institute for Puerto Rican Policy* 13 (April 1993): 2.

According to Felix Padilla, "Hispanismo or Latinismo represents a collective-generated ethnic group identity and behavior, that is, a type of identification and behavior which is produced out of the intergroup relations or social interaction of at least two Spanish-speaking groups." He describes the phenomenon as "a process through which two or more Spanish-surnamed ethnics cross their individual group boundaries and seek solidarity as a wider Latino unit."[3] This solidarity occurs to bring about political and sociological transformation when the conditions of life demand change.

Padilla goes on to say that the structural factors that produce solidarity are conditions which Spanish-speaking groups experience in common at the city-wide level, such as discrimination in education, employment and housing.[4] Therefore, the solidarity motivated from intergroup experience is for the purpose of forming a cohesive group structure for justice or social inequalities. However, the solidarity formation that is given from outside the intergroup experience, from non-Hispanics, is primarily for reasons of propagating social inequalities that relate to the labor market and other forms of discrimination. Nagel and Olzak explain:

> Competition for jobs in ethnically diverse labor markets tends to become organized along ethnic lines. This can occur when employers try to lower wages or break up labor organizing efforts by opening formerly segregated job markets, thus producing ethnic competition for jobs. . . . Or, organized ethnic groups themselves can attempt to corner job or commodity markets for purposes of economic advancement, thus introducing ethnicity into economic competition.[5]

The Federal Interagency Committee on Education defined *Hispanic* in 1975 as "a person of Mexican, Puerto Rican, Cuban, Central or South American, or other Spanish culture or origin, regardless of race."[6]

Isidro Lucas points to the variety of titles given by the U.S. Bureau of Census in counting this population—Spanish-speaking, Spanish origin, Spanish surname. He states that the consensus favors the term *Hispanic*, particularly in official circles. But he cautions that the name has an "administrative convenience."[7]

The term *Hispanic* is the clearest way to describe the Spanish-speaking, Spanish-surnamed people living in the United States. It is used in the Hispanic church (primarily the Roman Catholic church) as well as in official community support systems. Many do not believe the term *Latino* is helpful because it includes Italians, Portuguese and French. However, *Hispanic* is not necessarily well accepted by all subgroups either.

In some parts of New Mexico "Hispano" refers to the descendants of European-Spanish stock who never lived in modern-day Mexico. They are the original Spanish-speaking New Mexicans, who intermarried neither with the native Indians nor with the invading Anglos—the term applied to non-Hispanos from the United States. . . . Naturally enough the other groups of Spanish-speaking in New Mexico feel that the term "Hispano" excludes them.[8]

### How Many Hispanics Live in the U.S.?

Table 1.2 lists the Hispanic population in 1970 as 9,073,237. It grew to 14,608,673 in 1980, an increase of 61 percent, and to 22,354,059 in 1990, an increase from 1980 of 53 percent. Comparable increases for non-Hispanic blacks were 17.6 percent and 13.1 percent, while non-Hispanic whites[9] increased only 6.2 percent

**Table 1.2: Comparative Growth of U.S. Population Subgroups**

| Population Subgroup | Population 1970 | Population 1980 | Growth Rate 1970-1980 | Population 1990 | Growth Rate 1980-1990 |
|---|---|---|---|---|---|
| Total | 203,210,158 | 226,545,805 | 11.5% | 248,709,873 | 9.8% |
| Hispanic | 9,073,237 | 14,608,673 | 61.0% | 22,354,059 | 53.0% |
| Black | 22,539,362 | 26,504,985 | 17.6% | 29,986,060 | 13.1% |
| White | 178,119,221 | 189,079,281 | 6.2% | 199,686,070 | 5.6% |

Sources: Hispanic Policy Development Project, *The Hispanic Almanac* (New York: Hispanic Policy Development Project, 1987), p. 22; U.S. Bureau of the Census, 1990 Census of Population and Housing, Summary Tape File 1C (CD90-1C), February 1992.

and 5.6 percent in the same time periods. Therefore, the Hispanic population is not only large but is also growing at extremely high rates.

There is much controversy over the accuracy of the census figures. For one thing, they do not include the more than three million Puerto Ricans who live in Puerto Rico (and, as such, are citizens of the United States). Further, Hispanic leaders have long felt that the Bureau of the Census has underrepresented their numbers. Lucas listed the following possible reasons for what has been criticized as the 1970 census undercount of Hispanics:

> Lack of bilingual questionnaires; complicated census forms; absence of bilingual census takers or enumerators; the basic reliance on commercial, post office users, and telephone master lists; reluctance of communities to provide government with information because of distrust of all government activities; and underlying all of these reasons, the lack of a meaningful civic education campaign to alert the Latino population to the need, confidentiality, and usefulness of Census responses.[10]

Raymond Rivera, former national secretary for Hispanic ministries of the Reformed Church of America, also questions the accuracy of census data. "Despite improved census methods," he said, "many experts believe there was still an undercount in 1980, and that the Hispanic total (including Puerto Rico) is closer to 20 million."[11] The concern for undercounting was also expressed after the 1990 census.

### Where Do U.S. Hispanics Live?

Cities, with their ethnic diversity, high population density and quantitative growth, provide the living "quarters" for most Hispanics in the United States. Cities in themselves are not unfamiliar to Hispanic families, but U.S. cities bring a cultural clash that often leads to fear and polarization.

González indicates that "in 1980, 50 percent of all Hispanics lived in central cities, with an additional 37 percent living in metropolitan areas outside the central cities, for a total of 87 percent urban dwellers."[12] By the 1990 census, this percentage of urban U.S.

Hispanics had grown to 91.4. Such high numbers lead us to believe that most of those who were missed in the census reports were also urban.

By focusing on the twenty largest U.S. Hispanic metropolitan areas in 1980 and 1990, we can see the growth patterns (table 1.3). Not only must we consider the *numerical* increases in population but also the amazingly high *percentage* increases—over 100 percent in three metropolitan areas.

## Age and Family Structure

The growth of the Hispanic population has made the United States the fifth largest Spanish-speaking country in the world.[13] The federal government has described the dynamics of this expansion as follows:

1. *Hispanics are young:* Half are 20 years of age or younger, compared to a median age of 30 for the U.S. population as a whole. One out of every 8 Hispanics is five years of age or younger, compared to one out of every 13 in the total population.

2. *Hispanics are fertile:* The fertility rate of Hispanics is double that of whites and blacks—about 1.8% natural increase per year compared to 1% for the rest of the population.

3. *Hispanics have large families:* Government statistics show Hispanic families with an average of 4.29 members compared with 4.11 for blacks and 3.49 for whites. Only 5% of all American families consist of seven or more persons, but 11% of Hispanic families equal or exceed that number. Among Mexican-Americans, the largest Hispanic group, 15% of the families have seven or more members.

4. *Hispanics come from conservative roots:* The overwhelming majority of Hispanics come from conservative religious backgrounds, making them less receptive to birth control measures and more opposed to abortion than the general population. Furthermore, Hispanic culture embraces early marriage and large families.[14]

## Table 1.3: The Twenty Largest U.S. Hispanic Metropolitan Areas

| Metropolitan Area | Rank | 1980 Hispanic Pop. | Rank | 1990 Hispanic Pop. | 1980-1990 Pop. | % Change |
|---|---|---|---|---|---|---|
| Los Angeles-Long Beach, Calif. | 1 | 2,066,103 | 1 | 3,351,242 | 1,285,139 | 62.2% |
| New York, N.Y.-N.J. | 2 | 1,493,148 | 2 | 1,889,662 | 396,514 | 26.6% |
| Miami, Fla. | 3 | 580,994 | 3 | 953,407 | 372,413 | 64.1% |
| Chicago, Ill. | 4 | 580,609 | 4 | 734,827 | 154,218 | 26.6% |
| San Antonio, Tex. | 5 | 481,511 | 7 | 620,290 | 138,779 | 28.8% |
| Houston, Tex. | 6 | 424,903 | 5 | 707,536 | 282,633 | 66.5% |
| San Francisco-Oakland, Calif. | 7 | 351,698 | 11 | 506,361 | 154,663 | 44.0% |
| El Paso, Tex. | 8 | 297,001 | 12 | 411,619 | 114,618 | 38.6% |
| Riverside-San Bernardino-Oakland, Calif | 9 | 290,280 | 6 | 686,096 | 395,816 | 136.4% |
| Anaheim-Santa Ana-Garden Grove, Calif. | 10 | 286,339 | 8 | 564,828 | 278,489 | 97.3% |
| San Diego, Calif. | 11 | 275,177 | 10 | 510,781 | 235,604 | 85.6% |
| Dallas-Fort Worth, Tex. | 12 | 249,614 | 9 | 518,917 | 269,303 | 107.9% |
| McAllen-Pharr-Edinburg, Tex. | 13 | 230,212 | 14 | 326,972 | 96,760 | 42.0% |
| San Jose, Calif. | 14 | 226,611 | 15 | 314,564 | 87,953 | 38.8% |
| Phoenix, Ariz. | 15 | 199,003 | 13 | 345,498 | 146,495 | 73.6% |
| Denver-Boulder, Colo. | 16 | 173,773 | 19 | 211,005 | 37,232 | 21.4% |
| Albuquerque, N.M. | 17 | 164,200 | | 178,310 | 14,110 | 8.6% |
| Brownsville-Harlingen-San Benito, Tex. | 18 | 161,654 | 18 | 212,995 | 51,341 | 31.8% |
| Corpus Christi, Tex. | 19 | 158,119 | | 181,860 | 23,741 | 15.0% |
| Fresno, Calif. | 20 | 150,790 | 16 | 236,634 | 85,844 | 56.9% |
| Washington, D.C. | | 93,380 | 17 | 224,786 | 131,406 | 140.7% |
| Newark, N.J. | | 132,372 | 20 | 188,299 | 55,927 | 42.2% |

Sources: Frank D. Bean and Marta Tienda, *The Hispanic Population of the United States* (New York: Russell Sage Foundation, 1987), p. 150. U.S. Bureau of the Census, 1990 Census of Population and Housing, Summary Tape File 1C (CD90-1C), February 1992.

Further, a full 34.9 percent of Hispanics are under age 18, compared to 25.4 percent for non-Hispanics, while only 5.1 percent of Hispanics are age 65 or over, compared to 12.8 percent for non-Hispanics.[15]

## Economics

Not only is the Hispanic community young, but the number of its households headed by women with no husbands is increasing—to 23.8 percent in 1991. The Puerto Rican sector had the highest percentage, 43.3 percent, and Mexicans had the lowest, 19.1 percent.[16] This phenomenon, combined with low occupational and wage structures, adds to the growing problem of Hispanic poverty.

In 1990 the average family income for non-Hispanics was $43,735 while the average family income for Hispanics was only $29,311.[17] This means that the average Hispanic family earned over $14,000 less in 1990 than the average non-Hispanic family. But since Hispanic families are larger than non-Hispanic families, the family income for Hispanics must service more people, which accounts for an even lower per capita income than the official figures suggest.

In spite of so much poverty, however, the Hispanic community in the United States has more buying power than all 73 million people in Mexico. This paradox explains in part why migration (documented and undocumented) continues at such high levels when conditions in the U.S. seem so negative for Hispanics.

Once they join the work force, Hispanics receive the lowest weekly wages of any major group in the labor market, with Hispanic women reporting the lowest wages. The result? A full 28.1 percent, or over 6 million Hispanics, lived below the poverty line in 1990, and 48.3 percent of Hispanic families headed by females were poor. The figures are even more harsh for Hispanic children under the age of eighteen, 38.4 percent of whom lived in poverty in 1990.[18]

The Census Bureau projects that the Hispanic community will have the largest increase in unemployment at 74 percent, while blacks and whites will maintain increases of about 29 percent and 15 percent, respectively. Currently, most Hispanic workers have blue-collar jobs. Only 13.2 percent of employed Hispanics serve in managerial and professional specialty positions, as compared to 27.8 percent of non-Hispanics.[19] Proportionately, less than half as many Hispanics hold these upper-level positions as do non-Hispanics. Table A1 in the appendix maps out the occupational structure of Hispanics compared to non-Hispanics.

Another dimension of the U.S. Hispanic economic experience is the stratification that has occurred among the various Hispanic groups themselves. Marta Tienda has shown that the "country of origin is an important axis for socioeconomic differentiation among individuals of Spanish heritage."[20] Understanding how economic stratification takes place will give us insight as to how the Puerto Ricans, Cubans and Mexican-Americans interface. It may also help us in the church to confront systemic evil and defend the rights of the present and future Hispanic people.

Still another dimension of the Hispanic economic situation is the ongoing decline of the Puerto Rican community's sense of well-being compared to that of Mexican-Americans and Cubans. Puerto Ricans have not been "preferred" workers in the United States, despite their unrestricted access and legal privileges as citizens of the U.S. Apparently citizenship status alone has little or no influence on the economic well-being of a people.

**Education**
Closely related to economics in shaping the future of the Hispanic community is education. Without sufficient education there will be no significant change in the income and employment dilemma. Unfortunately, Hispanics lag far behind non-Hispanics in achieving average educational skills. Table 1.4 indicates that only 51.3 percent of Hispanics completed four or more years of high school, compared to 77.3 percent of the total population in 1991.[21]

The dropout rate among Hispanics is at least three times higher than non-Hispanic whites, and they also drop out earlier, no later than spring semester of their sophomore year, according to

Petrovich.[22] One reason for the high dropout rate is the scarcity of Hispanic teachers in elementary and secondary schools who can serve as role models. Petrovich notes that "Hispanics contribute only a small fraction of the teaching force: 2.6% of elementary school teachers and 1.7% of secondary school teachers, respectively."[23]

## Table 1.4: Years of School Completed by U.S. Population Age 25 and Over, 1991

| Years of School | Non-Hispanics | Hispanics |
|---|---|---|
| Less than 5 years | 1.6% | 12.5% |
| 5-11 years | 17.9% | 36.2% |
| 12-15 years | 22.3% | 41.6% |
| 4 years of college or more | 58.2% | 9.7% |

Source: U.S. Bureau of the Census, Current Population Reports, Series P-20, No. 455, *The Hispanic Population in the United States: March 1991* (Washington, D.C.: U.S. Government Printing Office), p. 10.

### Language and Identity

Issues pertaining to language and cultural identity will also affect the future of Hispanic mission in the United States. "Spanish is clearly the second most important language in the United States. The 1980 Census estimated that 11,117,606 individuals, five or older, speak Spanish at home."[24]

Language in itself is neither a hindrance nor an asset. Those who have not held to the linguistic traditions are still committed to their cultural roots. There is a celebration of self and community focused on historic and distinctive realities. "I am not ashamed," yells a third-generation Hispanic woman whose friends confront her for not speaking Spanish.

A separate but related issue is that of identity versus assimilation. Hispanics have long occupied the communities of the U.S. without losing their identity. They have not followed the assimilation process of Swedes, Irish or Italians who have managed to join mainstream America. Hispanics are growing in their value and awareness of self. Few will accept any form of the "melting pot" notion.

Traditional theories of assimilation would lead to the expectation that Puerto Ricans born in the states would tend to be more assimilated.... But the pattern of racial self-classification of those born in the states did not differ radically from that of Puerto Ricans born in Puerto Rico but living in New York.[25]

Not only are Hispanics holding on to their cultural identity, but more and more of them are joining together to attack the problems of poverty, unemployment and underachievement in education. They are trying to do something about institutional racism and about their underrepresentation in community and state government. *Justice* is a common term among Hispanics who are confronting oppression and inequality.

## Hispanic Subgroups

As we have said, the U.S. Hispanic community is made up of various subgroups—Mexicans, Puerto Ricans, Cubans and other Hispanics. It helps to see the percentages of these subgroups in order to develop effective evangelistic strategies. Table 1.5 shows that the largest Hispanic subgroup is the Mexican-American, followed by other Hispanics, the Puerto Rican and then the Cuban-American.

In the table, "other Hispanics" represents a heterogeneous grouping of those that are not Mexican, Puerto Rican or Cuban and come from Central and South America, Spain, and the Caribbean, so they are excluded from most of the following comparative analyses. Although this group grew the least of all the subgroups between 1970 and 1980 (19 percent), it grew the most during the decade between 1980 and 1990 (66.7 percent). Members of this subgroup were geographically concentrated in 1980, but they are the most dispersed subgroup in 1990. This in part reflects the wide variety of national origins included in this category. Many of the individual national groupings are concentrated, but when combined into one category, the group is widely dispersed. Also, the economic conditions of this subgroup vary by national origin. Receptivity to many Hispanic national groups is complicated by

### Table 1.5: Composition of U.S. Hispanic Population, 1980 and 1990

| Hispanic Subgroup | 1980 | | 1990 | |
|---|---|---|---|---|
| | Number | Percent | Number | Percent |
| Mexican-American | 8,740,439 | 59.8% | 13,495,938 | 60.4% |
| Puerto Rican | 2,013,945 | 13.8% | 2,727,754 | 12.2% |
| Cuban-American | 803,226 | 5.5% | 1,043,932 | 4.7% |
| Other Hispanics | 3,051,063 | 20.9% | 5,086,435 | 22.8% |
| Total | 14,608,673 | 100.0% | 22,354,059 | 100.1% |

Source: Hispanic Policy Development Project, *The Hispanic Almanac* (New York: Hispanic Policy Development Project, 1987), p. 23. U.S. Bureau of the Census, 1990 Census of Population and Housing, Summary Tape File 1C (CD90-1C), February 1992.

the presence of undocumented people (due in part to the refusal of the U.S. to grant refugee status to those from war-torn nations).

### Comparative Growth

Comparative growth rates and numbers can be seen in table 1.6. Since the U.S. Census Bureau did not use the same enumeration criteria for identifying the Hispanic population in 1970 and 1980, caution should be used in analyzing the 1970-80 growth rates. However, the same criteria were used in 1980 and 1990, so the

### Table 1.6: Growth of U.S. Hispanic Subgroups

| Subgroup | Population 1970 | Population 1980 | 1970-80 Growth Rate | Population 1990 | 1980-90 Population Growth Rate |
|---|---|---|---|---|---|
| Total | 9,073,237 | 14,608,673 | 61.0% | 22,354,059 | 53.0% |
| Mexican-Amer. | 4,532,552 | 8,740,439 | 92.8% | 13,495,938 | 54.4% |
| Mainland P.R. | 1,429,664 | 2,018,945 | 41.2% | 2,727,754 | 35.4% |
| Cuban-Amer. | 544,627 | 803,226 | 47.5% | 1,043,932 | 30.0% |
| Other Hispanic | 2,566,394 | 3,051,063 | 18.9% | 5,086,435 | 66.7% |

Source: Hispanic Policy Development Project, *The Hispanic Almanac* (New York: Hispanic Policy Development Project, 1987), p. 34. U.S. Bureau of the Census, 1990 Census of Population and Housing, Summary Tape File 1C (CD90-1C), February 1992.

1980-90 growth rates are more reliable. As mentioned above, "other Hispanics" had the highest growth rate between 1980 and 1990.

Political unrest during the 1980s as well as severe economic distress in many countries caused higher-than-expected numbers of immigrants. Mexican-Americans grew by 54.4 percent between 1980 and 1990, followed by Puerto Ricans with a growth rate of 35.4 percent. Even the lowest growth rate of 30 percent by the Cubans still represented a large increase in population.

**Comparative Economics**

When we look at how Hispanics fare economically, we notice large differences in comparative median family income levels between the various subgroups (table 1.7). Puerto Ricans have the lowest median income, $18,008 in 1990. Puerto Ricans also have the highest percentage in poverty, 37.5 percent. Most of the subgroups had actually declined in terms of percentage of families in poverty from 1970 to 1980, but all the subgroups increased between 1980 and 1990. Cubans continue to have the highest median family income, $31,439 in 1990, and the lowest percent in poverty, 13.8 percent.

**Table 1.7: Percentage of U.S. Hispanic Families in Poverty by National Origin, 1970-90**

| Country of Origin | 1970 % | 1980 % | 1970-80 Change | 1990 % | 1980-90 Change |
|---|---|---|---|---|---|
| Mexican | 26.8 | 21.4 | -5.4 | 25.0 | 3.6 |
| Puerto Rican | 28.2 | 33.4 | 5.2 | 37.5 | 4.1 |
| Cuban | 13.1 | 11.2 | -1.9 | 13.8 | 2.6 |
| Central/South American | 15.5 | 19.8 | 4.3 | 22.2 | 2.4 |
| Other Hispanic | 20.6 | 14.4 | -6.2 | 19.4 | 5.0 |

Sources: Frank D. Bean and Marta Tienda, *The Hispanic Population of the United States* (New York: Russell Sage Foundation, 1987), p. 354. U.S. Bureau of the Census, Current Population Reports, Series P-20, No. 455, *The Hispanic Population in the United States: March 1991* (Washington, D.C.: U.S. Government Printing Office), pp. 18-19.

**Comparative Education**

Another striking difference between the subgroups is in education. Completing a high-school education leads to job access and earning power. However, we have already noted that a large percentage of Hispanics do not finish high school. Mexican-Americans fare the worst in this category, with only 43.6 percent of those 25 years and over in 1991 having completed high school. Puerto Ricans had 58 percent, while Cubans had 61 percent. A similar pattern emerges among those 25 years and over who completed four or more years of college. Only 6.2 percent of Mexicans achieved this level, while 10.1 percent of Puerto Ricans and 18.5 percent of Cubans did.

In looking at education, we must also differentiate between those born in the United States (native-born) and those who are foreign-born. (When applied to Puerto Ricans, *foreign-born* indicates those born on the island as opposed to on the mainland.) Table A2 in the appendix indicates those who have, as of 1980, dropped out of the educational system before finishing high school. Interestingly, there are more foreign-born dropouts than native-born for all subgroups, but the differences in percentage of native-born and foreign-born dropouts by subgroup vary widely. Cubans show the least difference with 11.4 percent of native-born and 16.1 percent of foreign-born dropping out prior to finishing high school. However, Mexicans differ vastly in their educational attainment by birthplace—30.4 percent of native-born and 59.4 percent of foreign-born Mexicans drop out.

## Comparative Residential Segregation

One other major point of differentiation among subgroups deserves our attention: residential segregation; that is, the degree to which Hispanics are isolated from non-Hispanics. There are two common ways to measure segregation. One, the index of dissimilarity, indicates the proportion of Hispanics in a city or metropolitan area who would have to move for there to be an equal proportion of Hispanics and non-Hispanic whites in all census tracts throughout the area. Any index over .600 is considered very high. A second way is to estimate the likelihood of contact between a Hispanic subgroup and Anglos. This index indicates the probability that a member of the Hispanic subgroup would meet an Anglo in his or her own neighborhood. Table A3 in the appendix shows these measures for five major U.S. cities. Puerto Ricans in Chicago have the highest dissimilarity index (.805), followed by Puerto Ricans in New York (.723). Mexicans in San Antonio have the lowest probability of contact with Anglos, but Puerto Ricans in New York are almost as low. Bean and Tienda report that

> data on Hispanic-Anglo dissimilarity suggest a moderate level of Hispanic segregation overall, but with considerable variability between metropolitan areas. During the 1970s the four largest Hispanic communities seemed to be converging toward a common high level of residential segregation, with Los Angeles, New York, and Chicago beginning to approach the very high levels typical of blacks in American cities, while smaller communities . . . displayed relatively low levels of segregation more characteristic of European ethnic groups.[26]

By looking at a city such as Chicago—the only city that ranks among the top ten locations for all subgroups—we can see the differential segregation among the subgroups. Puerto Ricans are much more segregated (with an index of .805) than either the Mexicans (.640) or the Cubans (.671). Bean and Tienda concluded that "data from the 1980 census reconfirm the unique position [of high levels of segregation] of Puerto Ricans in American society."[27]

### How Will the Church Respond?

The Hispanic community in the U.S. presents a formidable challenge for those committed to evangelism and holistic ministries. Understanding the employment, education and family issues presented in this chapter provides us with some assistance in equipping the church for an effective and comprehensive mission task.

In a recent publication by ASPIRA, a national organization

concerned with Hispanic youth, education and leadership development, the top ten Northeast Hispanic needs were recorded. I believe these touch on the critical issues in almost all cities, though not always in the same order of priority.

### Top Ten Needs of Hispanics in the Northeast
1. Increase Hispanic school attendance and reduce dropout rates.

2. Increase quality housing for low-income Hispanics.

3. Increase the number of Hispanic voters.

4. Increase the representation of Hispanics in elected and appointed offices.

5. Increase Hispanic representation in administrative and policymaking positions at all levels of the educational system: superintendents, school boards, etc.

6. Promote the development of Hispanic leadership.

7. Increase the availability of training and support programs to facilitate the entry of Hispanic women, youth and unemployed persons into the work force.

8. Improve the delivery of health care in the Hispanic community for all age groups, from prenatal care to gerontology.

9. Increase the Hispanic community's understanding of the political process at the national, state and local levels.

10. Increase Hispanic representation on housing policymaking bodies; i.e., planning, zoning and housing boards.[28]

How will the church meet this emerging culture, which will be less conservative on religious issues than that of the first generation? The Hispanic community will be struggling not as much with Anglo power structures as with Hispanic power structures. Those who hold the economic and educational power will also capture the political arena and perpetuate a lower, oppressed Hispanic stratum. The poor will continue to be poor and the uneducated will only be educated minimally. Initially the questions of justice will have to be confronted from within the Hispanic situation.

Various contextual questions will also challenge the Hispanic Christian community. Because migration continues from Mexico, Central America, South America and the Caribbean, there will always be a need for traditional conservative churches that perpetuate the culture of the first generation. At the same time, the bilingual, bicultural situation as well as the English monolingual and bicultural dynamics will present a challenge to the evangelical and nonevangelical Hispanic community. It will be important for the Hispanic church to accept and equip this new generation.

The church must keep in mind that linguistics is only one cultural criterion. A youthful population that is trying to determine its identity and destiny will need sensitive Christians to assist it. In the process, the church will be challenged in its cultural traditions, its theological perspective and its ecclesiastical formation. It must wrestle deeply with the issues of contextualization. Theology's ability to transform all of life will be tested. When the church believes it is to be soul centered, its only responsibility will be challenged. The gospel will be relevant when it becomes the good news for all of life, for the totality of the people's historical situation.

# Chapter 2

---

# A Historical
# Exchange

Considering the impact that Hispanics have made on U.S. history and the significant growth predictions for the future, very little has been written concerning Hispanics as a group in the United States. The history and activities of the Hispanic people have been primarily communicated within each specific grouping such as Puerto Rican, Mexican, Cuban and those from Nicaragua, Honduras and Spain.

The population of the U.S. at the time of its independence was approximately four million people (3,172,000 whites and 757,000 nonwhites, mostly blacks). The majority of the people lived in rural areas, leaving only five cities with a population of more than 8,000.[1]

Spanish-Americans at this time greatly outnumbered America's English-speaking population. Alexander von Humboldt revealed that at the end of the 18th century the Spanish-speaking population was composed of 3.25 million whites, 5.5 million mestizos, 7.5

million Indians and 0.75 million blacks.[2] With such a large population, it was easy to see why the Spanish-speaking people would govern and control the remaining U.S. territory.

> The border of the Spanish empire extended to the Mississippi River. . . . Florida was a Spanish territory. (That area came into American possession between 1819 and 1821.) "New Spain," the present-day Mexico, extended far into what is now the American Southwest.[3]

By 1825, after serious conflict and war, the Spanish empire teetered on the edge of destruction. The disarray and instability made it impossible for the Latin American colonies to retain their political power.

How often we have misunderstood American history. We chart its beginnings from the settlement of Jamestown in 1607 but neglect to mention Santa Fe, the second oldest city in the U.S., which was founded in 1610. Though our history classes and textbooks seem to communicate that nothing of significance occurred in America until the Northern Europeans arrived, most of what America is all about took place from southeast Texas to southern California, including New Mexico, Arizona and parts of Colorado, Utah and Nevada. Historians and educators have clearly misrepresented how America developed and the significant role of Mexican-Americans in that process.

> The truth is that people lived on this land before the Anglos invaded and took their land away from them. They fought for their freedom, loved their children, cared for their families and old people, and practiced religions which produced more brotherhood and less hypocrisy than what I see among Anglos today.[4]

Justo González tells a humorous story about mistaken historical notions in a lecture at Columbia Theological Seminary:

> When I began teaching in Atlanta, Georgia, I opened my first lecture by telling my students that there was a time when Havana—not Savannah, Georgia, but Havana, Cuba—was the capital of Georgia. And then I went on to say, "Welcome, y'all

42

furriners." This was intended only as a joke, but it may also serve to point out a fact often forgotten: As far as time is concerned, it is not the Hispanic-American but the Anglo-American who is the newcomer to this country. Nineteen years before the British founded their first colony in the land that Sir Walter Raleigh called Virginia, the Spanish based in Cuba founded a city that still exists in Saint Augustine, Florida. And twelve years before the pilgrims landed on Plymouth Rock, the Spanish founded the city of Santa Fe, New Mexico.[5]

## Early Mexican-American History

Unlike the Cubans and mainland Puerto Ricans, Mexican-Americans were part of the early roots of the United States. If we include the early settlers who entered the Southwest from Spain via Mexico, their involvement in U.S. history spans six centuries.[6]

The first colonizing powers to set foot on American soil were the great religious imperialists who sailed from the shores of Spain. These infiltrators sought more than religious converts, however; they also wanted slaves and wealth. Spain's move to the north of Old Mexico was motivated by greed for the riches they would find in the lands of the Aztecs, Mayas and Incas. Sure enough, gold and silver were discovered in what have been called the Seven Cities of Gold. Sadly, the Spanish harshly exploited the Indians, imposing slavery on them and seizing their wealth. At the same time, proselytizing took place among those who had been captured and made servants of the Spaniard families.

## Mexican Independence

Over time, Spanish domination was severely tested by the continued battles with the Indians. Fierce attacks by Apaches and Comanches took a toll on the limited number of Spaniards then in control. Mexicans, influenced by the American and French revolutions, declared independence on September 16, 1810 (celebrated as Mexican Independence Day). By 1821 this continued distraction and stress eventually diminished the power and sovereignty of Spain in the Southwest territory.[7] Texas, the northernmost border of the New World under Spanish control, came under Mexican authority that same year. Finally, in 1824, the United States of Mexico was formed as a federal republic.

The region controlled by Mexico, which covered 2,000 miles from San Francisco to the border of Central America, was weaker than perceived by the land grants. Mexico was hindered by strife and war. Also, political instability brought about lack of governmental control.

> During the three decades that followed independence, Mexico passed through something like 45 changes of government, countless military rebellions, "pronouncements," coups, and several foreign incursions.[8]

During those years the relationship between the United States and Mexico was productive and friendly. Mexico based its constitution on that of the U.S. In spite of this excellent relationship, however, neither country understood the other's culture and values. Few Americans knew Spanish and few Mexicans had any command of the English language.

By the early 1830s, conflict over the policy and control of Texas (then a part of Mexico) created tension between Mexico and the United States. Mexico had set up a generous immigration policy for those moving into Texas from the U.S., but immigrants still entered illegally. Many were Germans, with a distinctly different style of living and farming.

> Mexico did not object to immigration, provided that the colonists would adopt Mexican citizenship, abide by Mexican laws, become Catholics . . . and pay taxes. . . . Foreigners, after all, had come to Mexico of their own free will; they should be obedient to the customs of Mexico.[9]

The American immigrants were stubborn, however, and held to their belief of inalienable rights as practiced in the U.S.

The growth and power structure of the Anglos eventually led

Mexico to close its border, which provoked further unrest among both Mexican and Anglo families who wanted independence from Mexico. When Texas proclaimed its independence from Mexico on March 1, 1836, the announcement not only prompted the battle of the Alamo but also raised questions about the sovereignty of New Mexico and California. "Thus in the beginning," González writes, "it was not Hispanics who migrated to this nation, but this nation that migrated to Hispanic lands."[10]

## U.S. Acquisition of Mexican Territory

The treaty of Guadalupe Hidalgo, signed in 1848, initiated a legal dimension to the ongoing history of northern New Mexico. Land-ownership was being defined, and from 1854 to 1880 the United States declared acreages under the common land-ownership to be government land. The procedure introduced a bureaucratic dimension too cumbersome for many to understand, and strenuous legal battles for the purchase of property ensued. Because of widespread illiteracy and distrust among the Mexican people, titles were legally defected without any major defense.[11]

> Those Mexican nationals who had clear title to the land, and who trusted the American government enough to stake their claims, retained their possessions. But most did not trust the new government, did not register their homesteads, and were therefore driven out by land speculators.[12]

This history of Mexico and its relationship with the U.S. has influenced and has been influenced by U.S. immigration policy.

> *Mexican Americans* are a composite of Spaniards and Mexicans who were either absorbed under Southwest expansionist policies or who immigrated voluntarily to the United States following the cessation.[13]

During the early 1900s, Mexican-Americans would become citizens by means of immigration.

The discovery of gold in California in 1848 significantly altered the situation for Mexican-Americans. The "gold rush" of non-

Hispanic Americans to the West led to a decrease in the Hispanic population percentage and an increase in racial prejudice against the Mexican communities.

The population analysis of Mexican-Americans begins with the U.S. census of 1850.[14] Based on the information gathered, 13,300 Mexican-born persons lived in the U.S. at that time. By 1910 they numbered about 220,000, a major increase. From 1910 through 1930 various industries such as mining and specialty farming were becoming big business. Many Mexicans from the higher, more professional strata came to the U.S. Indians, who were unemployed, also came to work in the fields. Mexicans in the U.S. came to enjoy a more comfortable life than their previously poverty-stricken communities provided. Why did they have such easy access to employment? Because Mexican laborers were paid at the lowest wage level.

> Mexican laborers did most of the railway construction and maintenance work in southern California, New Mexico and Nevada, where they were willing to work for a lower wage than other immigrants. (The Southern Pacific Railroad in 1908 paid Greek section hands $1.60 per day; Japanese, $1.50; and Mexicans, $1.25.)[15]

In the agricultural industry, Mexicans were the most valuable ethnic group. Since the demand was great for laborers who would work for low wages, the Mexican labor force grew.

**The Effect of U.S. Industrialization**
World War I brought about more change in the Mexican-American community. The industrial development period created a labor market for Mexican-Americans in major manufacturing centers such as Chicago, Detroit and Milwaukee. As they moved to the cities, Mexicans became more Americanized, and a middle-class Mexican-American stratum began to form. Many Spanish-speaking Americans also joined the armed forces, which furthered the process of assimilation and economic growth. But many biases and

prejudices against Hispanics remained, making life conditions difficult.

Chicago became one of the most important Mexican communities. In 1916, 200 railroad track workers were hired. "The 1920 census counted twelve hundred Mexicans in the city, most of whom worked for the railroads, steel plants, and meat-packing houses."[16] Here began the Mexican-American growth pattern in the U.S. In 1930 the Chicago population of Mexican-Americans and Mexicans was 20,000. Within the next ten years this population had grown to 35,000. Mexicans tended to live near their place of work. The housing was poor, and the jobs were those left by earlier immigrants (East European, German and Scandinavian).

It is not as happy and gay a life as it is in Mexico. They have no fiestas or serenatas and no places for paseos [walks] in the evening. If you walk in the streets [of Chicago] in the evening, you suffer insults from uncouth persons. . . . It is very cold here in the winter. . . . In the summer it is too hot. The life here is very cheerless in contrast to Mexico. The neighbors are other nationalities and they are very hostile instead of friendly.[17]

The numbers continued to increase until the Great Depression, when the U.S. adopted a program of repatriation. This program involved forcing more than 400,000 Mexicans to return to Mexico, even if they were born in the U.S. "Indigence, not citizenship, was the criterion used in identifying Mexicans for repatriation."[18]

At the start of World War II, the U.S. once again needed laborers, and enacted the *braceros* program in 1942. This was an agreement in which Mexico provided the U.S. with agricultural workers. The U.S. subsidized the program by picking up the travel costs and giving certain wage and treatment guarantees. Although the program ended in 1964, it provided the impetus for linking communities in Mexico "with daughter settlements in the United States."[19] Further, it established the basis for a "modern network migration . . . and the number of family connections grew."[20] In other words, the social bases for migration became mature enough so that the migration process became self-sustaining. Although the U.S. set annual immigration quotas of 120,000 in 1964, there was no way to curtail the migration flow. By 1970 the number of immigrants had swelled to almost 750,000 annually, many of whom were undocumented. Because of this great (and ongoing) influx of Mexican-born, as well as the frequent return of U.S. Mexicans and Mexican-Americans to Mexico, the assimilation process has been and continues to be extremely slow.

> Mexicans and Puerto Ricans in the United States are here because of the territorial expansion of past generations of North Americans. Their lands have been taken from them and annexed to the United States, and their citizens have been guaranteed rights under treaties with our government; these treaties have often been broken or ignored, and the people have been forced to assimilate "American ways" to exist.[21]

### Early Puerto Rican History

Puerto Ricans made their entrance into the U.S. through a different process. Before the second voyage of Columbus to the New World and his discovery of Puerto Rico in November 1493, the island was inhabited by Arawak Indians from South America. Puerto Ricans are descendants of those Indians, the Spaniards who colonized the island, and black slaves brought in by the Spaniards. Within a short time the original population was wiped out.

### Americanization of Puerto Rico

On July 25, 1898, U.S. troops led by Admiral George Dewey invaded Puerto Rico and seized control from the Spanish. The army overtook one of the ports, and within three weeks forcibly occupied one-third of the island. Dewey felt the island must be occupied by Americans for strategic purposes. However, Americans not only occupied the island, but through their expansion policies they reduced it to a welfare state and a dependent country.

This Americanization process resulted in many changes, most

notably the reform of the educational system. Public schools were no longer able to operate because of the war. Teachers were not being paid; therefore, they returned to Spain. Twelve days after the American flag had been raised, the school system was based on the form and philosophy of the United States. The new school arrangement had one interesting feature: In order to receive an education, one had to accept U.S. citizenship and identify with the goals of the country. Schools immediately made it a priority to hire English-speaking teachers.

Through the years schools were named Washington, Franklin and Jefferson, and U.S. holidays were observed. The system, and particularly the commissioner of education, wanted to make Puerto Rican children into good Americans. The American flag, the pledge of allegiance and other forms of patriotic fervor were imposed throughout the island.

Clara Rodríguez opens her book *Puerto Ricans Born in the U.S.A.* by stating,

> Since 1898, all Puerto Ricans have been born in the U.S.A., for that was the year that the United States invaded Puerto Rico as part of its war with Spain and proceeded to make Puerto Rico an unincorporated territory of the United States.[22]

However, under U.S. government and policies, the people of the island actually experienced less autonomy than they had under Spain. America's cultural invasion has had and continues to have a tremendously negative effect on the people of Puerto Rico.

**Commonwealth Status of Puerto Rico**

When Puerto Rico became a commonwealth in 1952, many believed that the people's sense of autonomy and well-being would improve; but it did not. The substance of its relationship to the U.S. was still colonial rule. The people of Puerto Rico are not free to determine their own foreign policy, and therefore cannot establish laws for the immigration process.

At present, Puerto Rico is represented in the U.S. Congress by a resident commissioner who *cannot* vote. Puerto Ricans who are residents of Puerto Rico also cannot vote in national elections.[23] Major difficulties occurred in the economic development of U.S. interests in Puerto Rico. The development process discouraged indigenous economic formation. Exploitation and discrimination prevailed. In 1947 Operation Bootstrap was initiated through the efforts of Luis Muñoz Marín, who, in 1948, became the first governor of Puerto Rico elected by the people rather than appointed by the U.S. government. Operation Bootstrap led to immediate industrialization and urbanization and was forever changing the complexion of the island. More and more Puerto Ricans moved to small cities, and by 1970, 60 percent would live in urban areas. The image of Puerto Ricans as agrarian people ceased.

### Puerto Ricans on the Mainland

When Puerto Ricans decided to migrate to the mainland, they were most likely to move to New York City; they now constitute more than 60 percent of the city's Hispanic population. This migration actually began in the early 19th century, but the three major phases of migration from Puerto Rico occurred in the 20th century. The first took place from 1900 to 1945, and these people were called *pioneers*. Many of them settled in New York. The second major move, much larger than the first, occurred from 1945 to 1964. Again, most went to New York and expanded the boundaries of the earlier pioneers. The third movement from Puerto Rico came from 1965 to the present. This period is marked by a coming and going between Puerto Rico and the U.S. mainland, or, as historians have noted, "the revolving door migration." As these immigrants moved to other parts of the U.S., population percentages shifted until there were more Puerto Ricans living outside of New York State than in it.[24]

The discrimination shown toward Mexican-Americans also occurred toward Puerto Ricans. They live in the most undesirable areas of New York and work the lowest-paying jobs. The tensions internalized by Puerto Ricans come from the mixed messages they receive in the U.S. They entered this country under the banners of pluralism and assimilation. But once they arrived, they noticed that people in the U.S. had difficulty in tolerating differences. Mainland Americans segregated their society into whites and nonwhites and supported separate schools, jobs and housing for those racially or ethnically different.[25]

Most of us were taught everything we know about the history of Puerto Rico in—at best—a passing remark by a teacher who is using a textbook with only one paragraph on Puerto Rico. We were never told that the U.S. policy of citizenship and commonwealth is a joining of conquest and imperialistic purposes. Puerto Rico at present is politically and economically dependent. How surprised we are when we realize that the plight of Puerto Ricans parallels the experiences of people from other colonized countries such as Algeria, Tunisia, Morocco and West or East India who have migrated to English, French or Dutch "fatherlands."[26]

Puerto Rico sustained four centuries of Spanish colonization until the invasion of the United States and thus retains many Spanish elements in its culture. It has now completed almost a full century of having a similar relationship with the United States. Many still strive for the independence of Puerto Rico, wanting an end to outside exploitation. The ambiguity Puerto Ricans face as citizens without full rights or representation influences their ability to participate in the opportunity structures normally open to citizens. This must be understood to effectively develop ministries among them.

## Cuban Historical Background

The first exploration of what is now Florida was conducted by Ponce de Leon, who was based in Puerto Rico and who journeyed to Florida in 1513. Since Florida was in one sense considered part of the Spanish Caribbean, many were familiar with the territory. The Spanish were guided by their lust for gold, which was supposed to be available in Florida. While attempting to settle in Florida, Ponce de Leon received a serious wound (from which he would later die) and returned to Cuba. But his colorful stories may have prompted some Cubans to move to the United States. The first wave of Cuban immigration began when Spain was forced to cede Florida to the United States in 1821, and it continued at a slow pace until 1950. The second and largest wave followed Fidel Castro's takeover of Cuba in January 1959, when approximately 300,000 Cubans left for the United States. More recently, the Mariel boatlift brought another 125,000 Cubans between April and October of 1980.

A major ingredient in the development of U.S.-Cuban relations and the establishment of Cuban communities in the Gulf and Atlantic coastal cities of the U.S. was the economic and commercial growth of those cities. Another important factor was political dissatisfaction in Cuba.[27] Like Puerto Rico and Mexico, Cuba has felt the strong domination of foreign countries. Spain ruled from 1511 to 1898, and slavery was a lucrative trade. Many Cubans, seeing what had happened to Santo Domingo and Haiti after their black populations had become the majority, feared that Cuban cultural identity would be destroyed. A strong abolitionist movement formed. "The reform movement of the 1830s had championed the abolition of the slave trade, and within a decade some had even suggested a gradual indemnified abolition," Poyo writes.[28] Cuba was a vulnerable nation, and many other nations wanted it. Neither the British, French or U.S. wanted each other to have authority or control over Cuba.

Cubans began migrating to the eastern cities of the U.S. as early as 1820. As with the Puerto Rican community, many settled in New York. During the 1880s, many Cubans migrated to Florida. This exodus reflected Cuba's weakening economy, due in part to the destruction of Cuban plantations during the war.[29] As the economy failed and unemployment and economic difficulties increased, emigration to New York, Key West and Tampa increased. This migratory flow was also encouraged by a growing and successful economy in Florida. By 1885 nearly one hundred Cuban-controlled Key West cigar factories employed some 3,000 workers. At the end of that decade, the industry in Key West produced about 100 million cigars annually.[30]

"From 1865 until 1898 Cuban history is primarily a chronicle of political and economic woes interspersed with rebellions," Boswell and Curtis write.[31] In 1878, the Ten Years' War ended in an ineffectual truce. However, Antonio Maceo and Maximo Gómez had emerged as leaders, along with José Martí, a young poet who organized revolutionary efforts in Havana. In 1879, after being deported to Spain, Martí went to New York City for fifteen years, where he continued his revolutionary involvement by organizing money, arms and recruits for another attempt at independence from Spain. Declining economic conditions in Cuba caused a great deal of dissatisfaction, and the revolution began in 1895. Martí returned to Cuba and lost his life in the struggle, as did Maceo, but the revolution continued.

The U.S. recognized the seriousness of the struggle in 1898, and sent the battleship *Maine* as a precaution. When it blew up, the U.S. declared war on Spain, and four months later signed an armistice with Spain. Cuba received independence with some conditions, but the Cubans fighting the revolution were ignored by the U.S. Martí's influence remained, however. Shorris writes, "José Martí affected the politics of his country forever, but in a man such as he it is the moral influence that is, in the end, profound. . . . Cuba developed a strong intellectual tradition."[32]

From 1898 to 1902 the U.S. military occupied Cuba. However, Cuba resisted and obtained its independence in 1902. The cost of this independence was the establishment of Guantanamo Bay Base, occupied by Americans, and the Platt Amendment, which permitted the U.S. to intervene in the internal affairs of Cuba. Cuba was tied to the U.S. in many ways, especially economically, until 1959.

Economics always plays a significant role in the welfare of a country. Cuba, a basically agrarian country depending on one crop (sugar) and its partnership with the United States, was vulnerable. Industrial development was limited. In 1952 a coup d'etat by Batista, who came from a modest background, failed to inspire the Cuban people. Some changes did occur with him, however, and by 1958 the agricultural value of the country had grown to $734 million, of which refined sugar was $452 million. But many difficulties remained, caused by poverty and an uneven rate of development. "Cuba, at the time of Fidel Castro's takeover, . . . remained in an essentially underdeveloped condition."[33]

### Castro's Takeover

After Castro and communism overtook Cuba in 1959, Cuba became economically dependent on the Soviet Union and other communist countries.[34] A "new class" was developed, and many Cubans left the country. They sought help and refuge in Spain, Mexico and Puerto Rico, but the majority turned to the United States, which became the land of hope for many Cubans.

> Overall, the newcomers to the United States tended to be better educated than those of their countrymen who remained behind, although the pattern began to change during the mid-1960s.[35]

After the Castro revolution, the number of Cubans residing in the U.S. mushroomed from approximately 40,000 to more than 1 million.

> In the period since the revolution no other country has contributed more refugees seeking exile in the United States, and only Mexico has contributed a greater number of emigrants to this country.[36]

Because those who initially came to the U.S. after the Castro takeover had above-average education and entrepreneurial skills, the economic base for Cubans would move more quickly up the ladder of success. Politics and major corporations were affected by this significant stratum of the Cuban community. The Cuban people have been careful in their assimilation and have successfully retained their cultural and ethnic heritage.

One important characteristic of Cuban immigrants in the early 1960s was the feeling that their visit to the United States was temporary. They believed that Cuba would be liberated and that they would soon return. Their expectations of Castro's removal and their imminent return tended to block their stability and proper political representation and authority. As the Cuban counterrevolution movement failed, they began to realize that they must adjust to a new way of living. By the close of the 1960s Cubans were seeking American citizenship and taking a more serious role in American politics.

> In 1970 approximately 25 percent of all Latinos living in metropolitan Miami were United States citizens. By 1978 the figure had risen to 43 percent. Furthermore, of those who were not yet citizens, 77 percent planned to apply.[37]

As expected, the Cuban-American family has developed differently than in Cuba, but it still differs drastically from the U.S. nuclear-family concept. It still promotes traditional roles for men and women. Men are expected to go out to work while their wives stay home. The second generation, however, has been adopting certain Anglo attitudes and behavior patterns. Economic realities have led many women to work also, leaving the tasks of housekeeping and babysitting to the elderly. Marriages also changed as second-generation women wed non-Spanish men.[38] Along with these changes, we see in the U.S. census of 1980 that 95 percent of Cubans in the U.S. considered themselves Caucasians. Some U.S. sociologists have concluded that the major reason for immigration was the "search [for] a higher living standard."[39]

## Other Hispanics

In this book the analysis of Hispanics from other lands is limited. A recent book by Emilio A. Núñez C. and William D. Taylor provides a Latin American perspective but excludes the Commonwealth of Puerto Rico.[40] I believe that the Hispanic church in the U.S. will grow primarily, but not exclusively, through the leadership of Mexicans, Cubans and Puerto Ricans, each finding their niche in a particular denominational structure, whether formal or informal, that is more suited to their cultural ethos. But the signs are clear that increasing numbers of Hispanics from other lands are entering the U.S. When Congress lifted the traditional quota system and instituted a limit of 120,000 per year from the Western Hemisphere, the immigration movement increased. The U.S. remained an open society for those from Latin America.[41]

## Dominican Republic and Haiti

Immigrants from the Dominican Republic and Haiti found the poverty of their homeland too cruel to endure and entered the U.S. to work in cheap labor forces. Even though Haitians were primarily involved in poorly paid agricultural work, more and more they began to seek industrial employment. Because these immigrants were not U.S. citizens like the Puerto Ricans, they had to face additional ordeals. Dominicans at times claimed they were Puerto Rican for the purpose of immigration. Still others described themselves as Cubans for purposes of prestige.[42]

By 1980 more than 500,000 Dominicans lived in the U.S., mostly clustered in northern Manhattan. This grouping was formed not because of cultural conflict with Puerto Ricans, who lived in northeast Manhattan and the South Bronx, but rather for practical reasons of family and friendship support. Indeed, the Puerto Rican and Dominican communities had much in common.

## Central Americans

The immigration process for Central Americans and South Americans has been somewhat different. In part, the Central American movement toward residence in the U.S. was motivated by conflict and revolution. Approximately 500,000 immigrants from El Salvador (legal and illegal) had arrived in the U.S. by 1983. In Nicaragua the revolution of the early 1980s prompted 200,000 to leave their country for the U.S. The political arena was jammed with ideologies from Marxist-Leninist contributors to democratic hopefuls. The United States endured ongoing accusations of promoting "Yankee Imperialism." Oppression led to guerrilla warfare, which ultimately forced emigration on many Central Americans. Many of the dispossessed found shelter and a new life in Los Angeles, which today is the second largest Salvadoran city. The misery and pain Salvadorans faced in order to reach Los Angeles equals that of any such movement, including the "boat people." The "feet people" who marched from one border to another, risking their own and their families' lives, were courageous, determined people.

## South Americans

On the other hand, those who came from far south, from Chile, Argentina, Uruguay and other South American countries, had different forces with which to contend. Their immigration pattern resembled that of western Europeans at the close of World War II. The primary immigrants from South America were skilled, urban, middle-class people. Because of economic decline in their homelands, many hoped that the U.S. would provide a more promising environment for their families.

## Summary

We must keep in mind that Hispanics first came to this country not through migration but rather through expansion, purchase or military overthrow. Without question annexation has figured into this process. Even a quick look at a United States map reveals many cities and states with Spanish names—Florida, California, Nevada, Colorado, Los Angeles, San Francisco, San Diego, Sacramento. What does this tell us historically?

This brief overview can only provide an introduction to topics for further reading and study. I have provided it to remind us in the church of the importance of accurate information if we are to understand and minister to a people.

# Chapter 3

---

# Hispanic People
# in a
# New Context

*The evangelization of these young Puerto Ricans, difficult as it may be for any traditional missionary approach, may well hold the key to the future of Christianity in New York City.*[1]

This chapter introduces a subject not often written about in missiological or historical journals: the significance of second- generation leadership, present and emerging. As the urbanization process continues, we are faced with a mission directive that is both urban and Hispanic. Arroyo[2] correctly speculates that the key to effective Hispanic ministry may be found in this new generation, which lives in a trilingual (English, Spanish, urban) and multicultural world. To cultivate compassion for second- and third-generation Hispanics, this chapter will present several life profiles, beginning with my own family, and identify the principles relevant to ministry among these people.

## My Parents' Introduction to New York City

When my parents, Manuel and Luisa Ortiz, were in their mid-twenties, they left their home in rural Puerto Rico to seek a better way of life. They arrived in New York City in 1936 with no skills and no understanding of what lay ahead for them. This city, with a dense population and multicultural dynamics, would be their first urban experience. They were citizens and yet foreigners. Two years later I was born. I was a Puerto Rican, but I had no images of the island and its beauty. All I had to identify with was New York's urban culture and language.

My father could read English, but he had left school quite early because of the death of his parents. My mother, on the other hand, was a high-school graduate, fluent in Spanish and English. Hoping to find employment, they moved in with relatives who had preceded them (the custom then and now). Life was difficult and filled with many disappointments. Employment was not available for unskilled people, and most businesses would not hire Hispanics, especially those not fluent in English.

The urban setting also posed new problems which they were unprepared to handle. They saw the city as a cold and impersonal place. They had come from a friendly and supportive rural environment where their extended family had lived all their lives. Now, they lived on the east side of New York where the multitudes were coming in from many countries through Ellis Island. They were surrounded by Italian immigrants on the east and African-Americans and Haitians on the west. Neighbors were cautious with each other, especially if they came from a different culture.

The climate was also extremely different. My parents had never seen snow or experienced temperatures below 60 degrees. The weather added to their feeling of coldness about the community.

Another difficult aspect for those in my parents' situation was living with others. Although this was the custom, many problems arose when two or three families lived together in one two-bedroom apartment. It was especially painful if only one person was employed. Even with all the discomforts and limitations of this kind of living arrangement, many of these families maintained some sort of harmony. However, many adult men felt much stress because their responsibilities, which included providing for their families, were being challenged. The lack of employment—combined with living off other people—caused great damage to their ego and sense of identity.

## Growing Up in the U.S.

My friends and I also faced a complicated situation. We felt torn between two worlds: the one we experienced at home, and the one we faced on the streets. There were no bilingual programs in the schools, so the primary language, and the only language used in school, was English. No one at home spoke English, and hardly anyone my age spoke Spanish on the streets. The trade language was primarily English, yet it was important for the business community to be bilingual. It was interesting to hear an Italian grocery store owner speak in Italian and English and then also in Spanish when it was called for. The Puerto Rican community had not yet developed as an economic power. Many of the merchants only used English, and if families wanted to purchase furniture or a major appliance, they needed a translator. Usually children were used because of their involvement in the English-speaking school system.

As time went on, values and language aspects of my culture were being stretched into a new reality. The various ethnic groups tended to form cultural pockets that only came together in the public schools. Though I lived in a mixed neighborhood comprised of Hispanics, African-Americans and Italians, other areas were culturally defined. I was chased or robbed at times by Italians because I was Puerto Rican. I was a stranger in the African-American community because I was Puerto Rican. I had to make survival my top agenda every day.

As I grew older, I began to wonder about my identity. My parents seldom knew what was happening with me and my siblings because they were consumed with economic and family tensions. Many parents, including my own, maintained their cultural identity and avoided community tensions by limiting their friendships to those in the extended family. They simply made no new friends. Even now, after living in the U.S. for fifty-seven years, my mother and father still prefer the Spanish language both at home and in matters of trade and shopping. This has kept them within certain relational and social boundaries.

On the other hand, I realized that my generation felt the tension of a broader world in which we could retain our cultural roots but also create a new kind of life for ourselves. Our parents did not know how to provide the kind of support that would help us excel in school and in society. The best they could do was make sure we attended school every day and stayed out of trouble. No news was good news. How and what we achieved did not matter nearly as much as whether we behaved properly and respected authority.

During my preteenage years, the conversation in my home changed. My parents would speak to me in Spanish and I would respond in English. Eventually my parents' English vocabulary grew and they learned to speak with me in English, but they always preferred Spanish. Often they would remark that they wanted me to use Spanish, but when I did, they would correct my use of words. This further strained my continued use of the Spanish language. Again I felt caught between two worlds—one in which I could enjoy the strength and stability of my family, and the other in which I was confronted with my sense of identity and with my expectations for the future.

**Coping with Two Worlds**
In the community a new functional language arose that incorporated both worlds by juxtaposing Spanish grammatical structure on English-based words. Today that language is called Spanglish, and it permitted me and my friends to develop a unique identity within

the second generation. Our views, music, heroes and social activities were changing and at times separated us from our parents. The families realized that their children were not following their ways, that serious and sometimes offensive cultural changes were taking place. For example, my friends and I enjoyed both the Hispanic music we had grown up with at home and the contemporary music we heard in the community. But the adults made fun of this. Our parents felt we were betraying their culture and embracing another one instead. They viewed change as a denial of everything they believed, a rejection of everything they were. Conflicts flared up frequently between parents and children—sometimes subtle, other times quite confrontive. Children were forced to choose one world or the other, and their parents set the guidelines. If children wanted to accept the urban cultural experience they were born into, they basically had to repudiate their parents.

The community also drew lines between the newly arrived and those born in the United States. It soon became the second generation versus the first generation, us versus them. Those who were primarily monocultural and monolingual (first generation) soon turned against my friends and me. They would tell us we were not "true" Puerto Ricans, a designation primarily based on language and communication. In return we used the word *jíbaros* to describe those from Puerto Rico. Although *jíbaro* simply refers to a person from the mountainous farm regions or a rustic countryman, we used it derogatorily, with a meaning similar to the word *hick*.

**Where the Church Fit In**
Growing up in the Roman Catholic church, I found that it primarily concerned itself with meeting the needs of the newly arrived families and those who embraced the value system of their native country—rural, monolingual, embodying conservative Hispanic values. In other words, the church reinforced the paradox of living in two hostile worlds. The young people were excluded. Many of us could not fully embrace our parents' lifestyle and religious

beliefs and soon became indifferent to the church. In later years I saw this problem continue within Protestant evangelical churches. The evangelical Hispanic church in the U.S. was also primarily rural and embraced the values and traditions of the homeland. The second and third generations were also excluded, though they made some effort to assimilate. The young people who attended did so primarily because of their parents. When the parents did not attend, neither did the young people. This led many to reject the church out of either anger or apathy.

## Other Life Stories

Storytelling has had more impact on the Hispanic community than any other medium. It is in the narrative that we learn anthropology, sociology and theology. People have unique experiences that are too often kept as family history and never revealed to others. That is why I have related my own story.

It would also be helpful to look at other stories about real people (with names changed) representing each of the three main Hispanic subgroups in order to determine the differences and similarities in the experience of second-generation Mexican-Americans, Puerto Ricans and Cuban-Americans. We can then use what we learn to develop effective church programs. The significance of these narratives lies in their meaning to the reader. Therefore, let us move carefully through each story, attempting to discover the process of change and the struggle for identity in a new and often foreign context.

## María Chávez

María was born in Tamualipas, Mexico, but immigrated to Chicago with her parents at age three. (Her parents were then in their thirties.) She has three older brothers and one younger brother, who was born in Chicago. Her mother is a homemaker and child-care worker, and her father is a retired baker.

María lived in a Spanish neighborhood in Chicago and spoke

Spanish in her home. When she went to school, she remembers, she was regularly taken out of class for TESL (Teaching English as a Second Language) classes to learn English. She never thought she had an accent until Anglos started correcting her.

Although María was Mexican, she actually had to deal with three different cultures. She knew she was Mexican and related to that culture at home. But after third grade, she lived in a primarily Puerto Rican community, and all her friends were Puerto Rican, so that culture had a strong influence. The third culture came from a youth organization operated by Anglos. There she became a Christian at age nine and first learned about the Christian lifestyle. During her years in this group (which was geared toward reaching Hispanic youth), she simply accepted the way they did things. She did not realize there could have been a different approach until much later when she became involved in a Spanish bilingual church. At various times María struggled with her sense of identity, but now if she is asked, she will respond, "I am Mexican" (not Mexican-American, Chicano or Hispanic). Though she questioned herself, she never felt ashamed of her heritage. Even her younger brother, who was born in the States, identifies himself as Mexican because his parents are Mexican and they gave him that heritage.

María was a very capable student and went to a magnet high school. It was predominantly Anglo, and the Hispanics always sat at different tables. She realized that she had to take pride in her identity and yet still know how to work in the Anglo world. As time passed, she also noticed that even though Anglos were predominant, they were not always right (as she thought when she was younger).

In college María saw more of the differences. She could see the surprise in some of her teachers when she did well, and recognized their prejudicial attitude. Fortunately, she was not deterred from her goal, and now María serves as principal of a Christian inner-city Hispanic elementary school and a role model for her students.

In her church María has learned a great deal by observing its

65

involvement in the community. She will always be grateful to the Anglos who led her to the Lord, but she also can see how some things should have been different. She believes it is vital to retain the cultural and linguistic heritage in the church. "It should be something you're always proud of, even if you don't know the language as completely as you would like to," she says. Songs should be printed both in Spanish and English, and the worship should be lively to suit the young tastes of most second-generation Hispanics. A church should emphasize the uniqueness of all people and that God did not make a mistake by creating different races. We all should be proud of who we are. She wants the church to encourage its people to grow and move out into the world, but also to return and minister to those in their community. This offers hope of change rather than the despair of abandonment. "Because we have Christ," she says, "we are not only capable, but capable to come back to minister." She appreciates her church for opening her eyes to the needs of the community and for getting involved.

María's mother attends a Spanish monolingual church which is completely first-generation. There the children go with their parents when they are young, but when they reach their teens, conflict arises and many of them stop attending. The pattern highlights the need for churches that are geared to the second generation.

### Richard Rodriguez

A Mexican-American raised in Sacramento, California, Richard responded differently to the conflicts of identity than María. He wrote an autobiography[3] in which he deals with his journey as a second-generation Hispanic primarily through the avenues of language and education.

As a very young child, Richard was able to differentiate the "sounds" of language. At home where his family spoke Spanish, the sound was one of intimacy. This was the private sector of his life, and Spanish was used to establish his private identity. If anyone who spoke English entered his home or if, while going to a store or other outside place, his family encountered someone who spoke English, the whole sound of their speech changed, not just the language itself. English was a public language, and to be a part of the public sphere of life one had to learn English. However, to learn English well enough to establish a public identity, Richard had to pay a price.

As a child, Richard spoke Spanish and knew barely enough English to buy something from the store. He did not like English, not the sound nor the way he felt around those who spoke it. He took comfort in Spanish and in the intimacy of his family life as communicated through the Spanish language. Once he started school, however, his teachers advised him and his family to speak English at home so that the children would learn it better. The English they spoke was halting and strange to Richard, so that even though the family unit still contained the same people, he felt a tremendous loss in the intimacy they once shared. He fought learning English for some time, but finally accepted it.

Again and again in the days following, increasingly angry, I was obliged to hear my mother and father: "Speak to us *en inglés.*" (*Speak.*) Only then did I determine to learn classroom English. Weeks after, it happened: One day in school I raised my hand to volunteer an answer. I spoke out in a loud voice. And I did not think it remarkable when the entire class understood. That day, I moved very far from the disadvantaged child I had been only days earlier. The belief, the calming assurance that I belonged in public, had at last taken hold.[4]

Richard moved from loving Spanish and disliking the feeling he had when others forced his parents to speak English, to embracing English and being ashamed of his parents' attempts at the language, to eventually accepting their accent because he felt secure in his own public identity. Although he still understood Spanish, he spoke only English and described his Spanish-speaking skills as follows:

When relatives and Spanish-speaking friends of my parents came to the house, my brother and sisters seemed reticent to use Spanish, but at least they managed to say a few necessary words before being excused. I never managed so gracefully. I was cursed with guilt. Each time I'd hear myself addressed in Spanish, I would be unable to respond with any success. I'd know the words I wanted to say, but I couldn't manage to say them. I would try to speak, but everything I said seemed to me horribly anglicized. My mouth would not form the words right. My jaw would tremble. After a phrase or two, I'd cough up a warm, silvery sound. And stop.

It surprised my listeners to hear me. They'd lower their heads, better to grasp what I was trying to say. They would repeat their questions in gentle, affectionate voices. But by then I would answer in English. No, no, they would say, we want you to speak to us in Spanish *(" en español")*. But I couldn't do it.[5]

The purpose in going through this loss both of language and all it meant in terms of familial intimacy was to ensure his place in the public and his public identity. He describes language and intimacy as "the great themes of my past."[6] After a while he realized he had made an important discovery:

*Intimacy is not created by a particular language; it is created by intimates.* The great change in my life was not linguistic but social. If, after becoming a successful student, I no longer heard intimate voices as often as I had earlier, it was not because I spoke English rather than Spanish. It was because I used public language for most of the day. I moved easily at last, a citizen in a crowded city of words.[7]

Rodriguez's life was a paradox. He became fanatical about reading, and read constantly. He pushed himself to achieve in school. As he puts it,

A primary reason for my success in the classroom was that I couldn't forget that schooling was changing me and separating me from the life I enjoyed before becoming a student.[8]

Even in his religious life he sees changes. He grew up as *un católico*, having learned about the church through Mexican Catholicism.

Then, starting with an English-speaking priest who visited in their home, his Catholicism became more and more of an English experience, and it, too, lost its former intimacy. Even the appearance of the *gringo* Catholic church reduced its intimacy for Richard. Although he is still Catholic, the church does not hold the same significance in his life.

Another difficulty Richard faced was having a darker complexion than many in his family. He grew to be ashamed of being brown, ashamed of his body, afraid to deal with a social life with girls, and mostly afraid of being looked upon as a *bracero,* a man who worked with his *brazos,* arms, like the Mexican farmers or laborers. In college he finally came to grips with his shame and fear and tried to rebel by working for one summer as a laborer. But he soon realized that with his education and status, he could never truly be a part of the working-class Mexicans. He was now middle class, and had lost the working part of his background.

Even in writing his book Richard had to deal with his private versus public identity. His mother requested that he not write about his family because that was private and it was painful for her to have people come up to her and talk about her family's life. He had to go against her wishes because he felt it was important for others to know, but it made him a man of secrets. He was not able to discuss his work—his life—with his family because he knew that it would bring them pain. The loss of intimacy became even more acute.

### Issues for Mexican-Americans

Both María and Richard faced many of the same tensions regarding identity and how to "make it" in this country with its Anglo majority. Mexican-Americans must learn to adapt and in so doing face cultural schizophrenia.[9] Outwardly they play the Anglo game and inwardly continue in Mexican-American cultural norms. This culture wants to maintain its Mexican-American origins within the U.S. pluralistic society. Mexican-Americans are of mixed origins—

Indian and Spanish. They are "what José Vasconcelos calls the *raza cósmica* or the cosmic race: a hybrid taking the best from both Indian and Spanish cultures to produce a third stock better than the other two."[10]

Many Mexicans came to the U.S. as seasonal migrant workers and settled in small border towns. From these small towns they migrated to larger cities such as Dallas. Some worked in larger industries and settled as permanent residents within a large metropolis such as Chicago. The largest concentration of Mexican-Americans is found in Texas (28.8 percent) and California (45.3 percent), which shows the importance of the U.S.-Mexico border. "The two countries share twin cities, binational markets, and a long history of economic interdependence."[11] The switch from being a rural, agricultural people to being largely urbanized has led to major changes in cultural behavior.

### Pedro Rivera

When one speaks with Puerto Ricans about their lives, the issue of identity arises again and again. Who are they, who are they accepted by, and what are the criteria for acceptance? Puerto Ricans view and work out this issue in a variety of ways. Let's look at a few examples.

Pedro Rivera's parents migrated from Puerto Rico to Chicago two years before his birth. At age thirty-two, he is the thirteenth of fourteen children (including two adopted sisters), most of whom were born in Puerto Rico. His mother is a homemaker, and his father is a retired machinist.

Pedro's family, like many Puerto Rican families, had a wide range of coloring. His mother was very dark and was often identified as being black. Many of his brothers and sisters were also dark, but Pedro had a light olive complexion. The color differences confused Pedro, because on the one hand he felt different because he was brown and other children were white, but on the other hand he felt awkward around his siblings at school functions and around his mother in public because she was so dark and he was light. He had to endure stares and discomfort both ways.

His family spoke Spanish at home, and he never spoke English until he started school. In fourth grade his teachers told him, "You can't speak Spanish here. You have to pronounce things this way. You're in America now," and they made him very aware that he was different and not doing things right. But as he worked on his English, his Spanish suffered. When he would go home from school, his parents would say, "You're Puerto Rican but you can't even speak the language." This dilemma forced Pedro early on to face the question, "Who am I?"

Pedro also had to deal with his awareness of being a minority. He did not know how to identify himself. He could say, "I am a Hispanic," or "I am a Puerto Rican," or "I am a Puerto Rican from Humboldt Park" (a Chicago neighborhood). He felt all the classifications and, although they could be viewed as negative or positive, he usually interpreted them as negative. These three areas of complexion, language and minority consciousness combined to instill in Pedro a sense of self-doubt and insecurity. He found himself apologizing for who he was and where he came from. Even when the person he was talking to did not care, he would identify himself and feel bad, thus revealing his insecurity.

His feelings of being different and not accepted were intensified because of where he lived. He first lived on the south side of Chicago, which was primarily African-American. Then he moved into a Polish community (which was quickly changing to Hispanic) and found himself chased all the time by the Polish children. His brothers joined Puerto Rican gangs, which meant he could not go certain places where rival gangs or Polish gangs were. In high school people would still chase him and call him names. He felt cheated by the Anglos and victimized by their prejudice, and his anger toward them was reinforced during the 1960s when he saw on TV all that was happening in the African-American struggle for civil rights.

In his home Pedro's family retained close family ties. His parents were more traditionally Spanish than the children, but the children still consulted the parents regarding all major decision-making. Most conflicts between Pedro and his parents (and between his friends and their parents) occurred because the parents felt their children did not want to carry the torch of their cultural heritage into the future. Paradoxically, while parents believe the children want to assimilate, most second-generation Puerto Ricans want to keep the strong values of their heritage. Pedro feels that the first generation actually want to assimilate more than the second in that they seek better-paying jobs. But when the children try to study and focus on educational goals, the parents say, "What's the use of going to school? Where's the money at?" So many older children feel the tension between studying and helping to pay the rent or buy food. The problem often splits families.

Pedro became a Christian at age twelve and has been active in the church since then. He earned a masters degree and now pastors a church in El Paso. He sees that many second-generation people are avoiding the church and instead attending self-help groups with a mildly religious flavor. While church turns them off, they may get together to just talk about God. They do not merely want to be pacified by a nice sermon; they want to know how they can bring about change in their situations. They want to be socially conscious in a responsible way and look toward the future, not just the present. In order to be successful, a second-generation church must be able to show that Christ and the Christian life can help transform the community.

### Juan Colón

Juan, too, struggled with the issue of identity. His parents, both Puerto Rican born, migrated as teenagers to New York City, where they met and married. Juan grew up with his two brothers and one cousin who lived with his family throughout his growing-up years. Juan's mother was a school aide and his father a *bodega* owner. (A *bodega* is a family-run corner grocery store that has great cultural significance in the Puerto Rican community.)

Juan now lives in Philadelphia, holds an important leadership position within the city's council of Hispanic churches, and is married with a family of his own. As he looks at his current responsibilities toward the Hispanic community, he recalls the irony of his identity journey.

Throughout his youth, Juan did not want to speak Spanish. He viewed it as an inferior language and Puerto Ricans as backward people. He did not want to be like them. In essence, he negated his cultural heritage and became socialized enough into mainstream Anglo society that he could succeed in school. Later in life, when he reembraced his heritage, his educational success equipped him to be a leader among his people. Had he not experienced those early negative feelings, he believes he would have had early problems in school and been labeled a failure—as was the case with many of the other kids he grew up with.

His desire to create his own identity only partially succeeded in that he was constantly reminded that he was different. In his early school days, the Anglo kids always let him know that he was not one of them. At age nine he moved to black Harlem, where he was once again different and therefore "bad." He identified himself as culturally black, and did not really associate with other Puerto Ricans until high school and college. He looks back at the 1970s and admits that even Anglo students were trying to "find themselves," but it seemed more important for ethnic minorities primarily because they were told they were an ethnic minority.

Juan hopes that the Hispanic church can realistically meet the needs of the second and third generation. He sees the importance of using English in church services because so many of the children do not know Spanish; but he also wants much of the religious instruction in Sunday school to be done in Spanish as a teaching tool. Juan recognizes that culture as well as language should be addressed. The children must be taught to be Hispanic. Part of that, but only part, is teaching the language, which he sees as the bridge connecting them to their cultural and historical roots.

## Issues for Puerto Ricans

From these life stories, I hope we can understand and feel the pressures Puerto Ricans must face in this country and the various ways they respond. They are a people in tension—politically, economically, sociologically and psychologically. They are fiercely trying to hold on to their cultural integrity. They must face the realities of independence versus political control, extreme poverty versus continued imperialistic welfare, and cultural invasion versus a new identity in the wake of Puerto Ricanism (the issue of identity—who I am versus what will I be).

The political status of Puerto Rico continues to overshadow all other issues for Puerto Ricans in the island and in the United States. Ever since the United States invaded and forced its control on Puerto Rico, two alternative political formulas have been proposed to eliminate the oppressive colonial reality of the Puerto Rican nation: Independence or annexation/statehood. (It is increasingly clear that annexation/statehood, while making Puerto Rico an equal partner in the sisterhood of the federal union, as far as political and administrative structures are concerned, will not end colonialism but in fact intensify the process which would eliminate not colonialism, but Puerto Rican culture.)[12]

This confrontation of cultures, which has continued since the invasion of American forces, affects our present historical reality. At the forefront of the U.S. Puerto Rican community are aggressive people who search deeply for destiny, integrity and a new reality without paternalism. These people are becoming aware that history written from one perspective is not accurate unless the unspoken underside of history responds and sifts through the dominant culture. Rather than bring about justice, U.S. expansion since 1860 has sought to acquire commercial, industrial and financial hegemony in the Western Hemisphere, and, as a corollary, military bases necessary to maintain this hegemony.[13] Puerto Rican culture has been a casualty of that expansion.

In order to understand the present historical reality, it is extremely important that history be discussed from its relational inception. In other words, the United States's primary involvement with Puerto Rico and Mexico is imperialistic. Mexicans and other Hispanics are not the new immigrants, as Isidro Lucas states in his book *The Browning of America,*[14] but rather its early settlers, as Arroyo and Elizondo disclose:

> Mexicans and Puerto Ricans in the United States are here because of the territorial expansion of past generations of North Americans. Their lands have been taken from them and annexed to the United States, and their citizens have been guaranteed rights under treaties with our government; these treaties have often been broken or ignored, and the people have been forced to assimilate "American ways" to exist.[15]

Mainland Puerto Ricans are an urban people, with 96.2 percent of them living in cities. Since the early 1900s, most have come to their second "home," New York City. However, as economic declines have affected many northeastern urban centers, migrants are beginning to choose other destinations.

> Many Puerto Ricans have moved to cities in New Jersey and Connecticut within the New York metropolitan area, others have chosen to jump from New York to Philadelphia, Boston, Cleveland, Chicago, San Francisco, and other locations.[16]

This migration pattern has been influenced by the location of extended families and the basic need for employment.

The primary motivation for Puerto Ricans to migrate has been economic. Unfortunately, the oppression they experienced in the early 1900s and the limited development of skills for urban work has led many of them to turn to welfare as the only light at the end of the tunnel. Their economic situation in Puerto Rico had resulted neither from lack of agricultural potential nor self-determination, but rather from the process of U.S. expansionism.

After the take-over in 1898, American investors through the collaboration and support of the United States government began to transform Puerto Rico's multicrop agricultural economy into one which relied almost exclusively on a single cash crop. By 1940 a different change was made as light industry was introduced to replace agriculture as the mainstay of Puerto Rico's economy. And in the 1960s petrochemicals and similar industries became the structural foundation of the island's economy. All those changes only contributed in fostering the creation of a large mass of unemployed Puerto Rican workers. In fact, by 1940 immigration to American cities and other parts of the Caribbean represented an "escape valve."[17]

It is important to understand that the "escape" was prompted by U.S. imperialistic interests that ended up driving Puerto Ricans into a second phase of economic oppression—a system that would bind them in welfare, ghettos and an unjust labor market. The socioeconomic development of Puerto Ricans has been the lowest of all Hispanics. They have lived and continue to live in poverty.

Another notable characteristic is the dynamic mobility of Puerto Ricans. Because travel between Puerto Rico and the mainland is unrestricted, migration patterns are "punctuated by the *va y ven* (back-and-forth) migratory movement of many Puerto Ricans."[18] Not only does this pattern affect population numbers, but it "reinforces many links to the island, although it also reflects repeated ruptures and renewals of ties, dismantlings and reconstructions of familial and communal networks in old and new settings."[19] The character of the Puerto Rican people as well as their environment both in the cities of the U.S. and on the island has gone through enormous change. Net migration has decreased while the native-born U.S. population has increased. "In 1950, approximately 25% of all Puerto Ricans living in the United States were born there. In 1970, that figure was closer to 40%. At present, it is more than half."[20] This shift will continue to mold the character and socioeconomic status of the Puerto Rican people.

## Milagros Salvedo

Milagros was born in Cuba and came to the United States in 1971 when she was five years old. Her mother died two years later, so she and her two sisters and one brother lived with her father and her father's daughter by a previous marriage. Her father was a steel worker.

When asked about conflicts in her growing-up years, Milagros points to the irony that her father left Cuba to find freedom, and yet could not deal with that freedom once he had it. She explains that in Cuba, children, especially daughters, never thought of leaving home until they were married. Until that time, daughters rarely dated, but rather were expected to stay home and learn from the mother "how to be a good wife." They were encouraged to learn cooking, typing and reading, but not to go out. In this country they found a very different scene. Dating happened frequently, and her father found dating styles difficult to accept. Her father's frustration came out in words like, "If you were in Cuba, you wouldn't be doing this," or, "You wouldn't be driving in Cuba" (because access to cars was so limited). Her father tried to be very strict. In Cuba parents were held accountable for their children, but here when children turned eighteen, they could be on their own.

Milagros has extremely dark skin, and people usually think she is black until they learn of her nationality. She found acceptance among other Hispanics as soon as they heard her speak and realized who she was. Personally, she had few problems with Anglos while growing up, but she had a great deal of trouble with African-Americans. Apparently they resented her as they would an "uppity black" because she spoke a different language and even spoke English with a different accent. She said that African-Americans more quickly detected she was not one of them because of the way she spoke. She rarely felt accepted by them.

School was also a problem. She knew virtually no English when she came to Chicago. The schools had no bilingual program at the time, but she was removed from her regular classes for TESL

77

lessons. Besides the language barrier, she encountered problems with her teachers' expectations. They didn't know that her school system in Cuba had been more advanced than in Chicago. So she was ahead of the other second graders in math and writing. One time a teacher hit her on her hand for writing her name in cursive because she was still supposed to be using block letters. On another occasion she had a problem with another student, and her mother was called in to school. Her mother spoke no English at all, so Milagros had to do all the translating, even though she knew very little English herself.

As Milagros grew up, most of her friends were Puerto Ricans and Mexicans. She had very little experience with Anglos. Even when she attended a predominantly Anglo college, she had mostly Hispanic friends. There she discovered that Hispanics quickly knew she was Hispanic, and African-Americans figured it out after hearing her talk for a while, but Anglos had a difficult time. They would say to her, "How can you be Spanish? You're black." She would answer that she was Spanish because she was born in Cuba and her family was Cuban. She became very outspoken, and the college administration didn't like it. Because she looked black, they called her a militant, and because she was Hispanic, they called her a bigmouth. Although she struggled with the administration, she had little difficulty with her teachers.

In terms of self-identity, Milagros calls herself Cuban. She has earned a masters degree in social work and is now working for a social service organization in the community she grew up in.

Religiously, Milagros grew up Catholic. In this country, she struggled with the Catholic church. The Spanish mass had geared everything to adults so she could not relate to it, and she felt totally lost in the English services. As a senior in high school, she accepted the Lord and joined a local bilingual church. She would like to see a second-generation church use mostly English and yet not neglect its Hispanic origins. She would even like the different nationalities to be acknowledged so that she could be Cuban, not just Hispanic.

The various Hispanic nationalities have much in common, but they also have differences. She feels the church should be a place where second-generation people can accept much of the American way of life and yet not forget their Hispanic culture; it should be a place where both parts of their lives are accepted. Services cannot be completely in Spanish, but the people need to know that they can worship and communicate with God in either language. And lively, accessible music is especially important.

## Issues for Cuban-Americans

In 1990 there were 1,043,932 Cubans in the U.S., 97.1 percent of whom lived in urban settings. They are the most urban of all Hispanic subgroups. Before Castro's rule, the Cuban population was minimal in the United States, but it has now become a significant power and movement. Cubans are considered the second largest foreign-born minority in the country (Puerto Ricans are not considered foreign-born) and the third largest Hispanic group. The Cuban community has received a great deal of attention for its industriousness and determination. Other interesting aspects of Cubans as compared to other Hispanic subgroups are the relatively high proportion of elderly persons, high levels of educational attainment, and high levels of income, business ownership and affluence. The children, or second generation, are also advanced in social and economic matters and seem to be well-established, bilingual young people. One obvious tension is the decreasing numbers of first-generation Cubans, since Castro has for the most part forbidden emigration. The first generation has had a substantial influence on society, and it remains to be seen whether the second generation will assume this responsibility.

The impact of Cubans has been greater in the major metropolitan areas such as Miami, New York, New Jersey, Chicago, and to a lesser degree Los Angeles. When the initial wave of refugees came to the U.S. in 1959, they tended to settle in the south Florida area. The Cuban Refugee Resettlement Program brought about some dispersion. However, Cubans are beginning to return to the Miami area. In 1980, 58.5 percent of the Cubans lived in Florida, 10.1 percent in New Jersey, 9.6 percent in New York and 6.9 percent in California. The 1990 census figures indicate that 64.6 percent now live in Florida, 8.2 percent in New Jersey, 7.1 percent in New York and 6.9 percent in California.

Four significant factors account for the relative success of Cubans here in the United States:

1. Most Cuban immigrants were identified as white; therefore the barriers of racism were limited.

2. The economic status and professions of those who came in the 1960s (middle class, educated, having business skills and financial support) seemed to fit in well with the value system of the dominant culture in the U.S.

3. They abhorred Marxism and were eager to adapt to the U.S. political system.

4. They were offered good financial support and educational programs by the federal government in keeping with their refugee status.

## Principles Discovered

I have shared these life stories, including my own, to help us understand the issues faced by second-generation Hispanics in the U.S. I hope they cause the reader to think more deeply about the cultural, sociological and missiological issues and how they relate to God's interest in growing his church in this country.

The relationship between the first and second generations has long been discussed in cities such as Los Angeles and is extremely important to the church in the North American urban context. Clearly the second-generation Hispanic population in the U.S. is growing. How we work with that segment of the church is crucial to the furtherance of the gospel. Let us look at several general areas in which the church can reconsider its present agenda and make proper attitudinal and conceptual changes in its ministry.

## Identity

In a racist and complicated society, the matter of identity becomes all-important. Second- and third-generation Hispanics are committed to being Hispanic, but without having to maintain the historical and traditional formation of the church. They are not *new* Hispanics or even Neo-Ricans or Chicanos; they are Puerto Ricans, Mexicans, Mexican-Americans and Cubans. They must be given the dignity of their culture if they are to grow as balanced and progressive individuals in their present situation.

There are a number of indications that, as is to be expected, U.S.-born Puerto Ricans are adapting to North American culture at a much more rapid pace than those who have immigrated from the island. At the same time, however, this should not be interpreted in the sense of a total readiness for assimilation. In recent years, there has been a strong movement among the members of the younger generation to seek their roots in Puerto Rico, and to return to the island even if it is just to recover the language of their parents.[21]

## History

Second-generation Hispanics must know their historical roots. Providing them with true historical data will help them to understand who they are and how they should be perceived by outsiders. Historical misperceptions may prompt them to ask:

Why are Hispanics considered a "problem" for the country and the church when their presence in this country preceded the arrival of the *Mayflower* at Plymouth Rock? Why have the Spanish-speaking been so invisible to the American Church?[22]

The Hispanic historical information given to our young people ranges from nothing at all to inaccurate, misleading data:

History books downgrade the quality of the Spanish colonization; cartoons show a fat, mustachioed Mexican, sombrero pulled down over his eyes, sleeping in the middle of the day. Hispanics are perceived as inferior because they live outside the basic ethos of the North American republic. The tale has been so convincing that some Spanish-speaking have believed it themselves and have rejected their deepest traditions, including the Catholic faith, to become "red-blooded" Americans.[23]

The life stories we have seen indicate that understanding historical roots and cultural uniqueness is vital to individual growth. It also helps to consider both the historical influence of Hispanics in general and of the unique group (Cuban, Mexican, Puerto Rican, etc.) in the North American world.

Most historical overviews of Hispanics begin with a negative analysis. Montiel writes:

> Ortega y Gasset, the great Spanish philosopher, once said that man does not generally live his genuine life but rather a life defined by others in society. This circumstance leads to a state of crisis which he defined as "the transition which a man makes from a life attached to some things and supported by them to a life attached to another and supported by other things."[24]

He goes on to say that

> Mexicans in the United States are facing a crisis, for those things which they believe and are attached to have been continuously under attack. Their history, body of knowledge, and strategies designed to integrate them into the dominant society have, in the words of the Chicano philosopher Tomás Atencio (1972), "been derived from someone else's action." The attacks against their culture and language, the neglect and distortion of their history, the rejection and alienation from their mother country, and the external definitions of their existence must provide the perspective for understanding the Chicano in this country.25

## Understanding

Second-generation Hispanics must be understood anthropologically and sociologically so that the church can provide "room" for them to express their cultural dynamics. This will enhance the

82

process of contextualization and make the church more effective in its mission to the world. Failure to make "room" for this growing second generation may cause them to depart from the evangelical church.

The stories also indicate a negative psychological effect on many second-generation Hispanics. The lack of acceptance and understanding confused and angered them. They were excluded in most social and religious affairs. Providing sociological and psychological information will help the second generation to understand the dilemma and continue life in a healthy manner.

### Inclusion in Ministry

Second-generation Hispanics must be included in the strategy for outreach and emerging leadership. Most Hispanic churches find this second generation to be an enigma to their ministries. They hesitate to include the second generation, fearing the major changes they will need to make in the way things are done. Normally the church brings all Hispanics together and follows the will of the dominant group, usually the rural-oriented first generation. But now the Hispanic church must learn to look toward the future, ministering not only to the monolingual, monocultural, rural traditional people who will continue to flow into the U.S., but also addressing the urban, multicultural needs of the emerging second generation. From the stories in this chapter, it appears that the second generation understands this phenomenon and can provide help and leadership.

### Language

Second-generation people tend to believe that the primary determining factor of true Hispanic identity is language—do you speak Spanish and, if so, how well do you speak it? Maldonado-Denis disagrees, arguing that the issue is not whether we speak Spanish as a primary language or even Spanish in the linguistic mode of the first generation. The primary issue is whether we are thinking in North American ideologies.

> In this sense the criterion of who is Puerto Rican is not based on one's capacity to speak Spanish correctly . . . but is based on identification with the values representative of the struggle for the national liberation of Puerto Rico.[26]

M. Estellie Smith, in her study of the Spanish-speaking population of Florida, indicates that the Spanish-speaking category has very little cultural validity or is of little value in classification of Hispanics.[27] She cautions that linguistic categories are but one aspect of the cultural reality.

Whenever a new linguistic formation comes about, conflict arises over linguistic and syntactic changes. Most often those who create a new communication form are functionally bilingual and have been born or raised in a context other than that of their parents. For Hispanics the new form has been called *Spanglish.*

When the first generation of Puerto Rican immigrants came to the United States, their native Spanish came into contact with English. As part of the process of adaptation to the new environment, there were objects, functions and new experiences that could not be expressed in the immigrant's language or were better expressed in English. Consequently, Spanish speakers began to borrow certain lexical items from English and to incorporate them into their own speech by applying Spanish phonological and morphological rules to them. This is how words and phrases such as *la factoría* (the factory) and *el rufo* (the roof) came into existence.[28]

Many have chastised the Hispanic second generation for doing something that actually began with the first immigrants from Puerto Rico, Cuba and Mexico. Some outspoken Hispanics such as Carlos Varo call this phenomenon a "chronic disease."[29] Others view it as deficient or sloppy Spanish. In any case, there is a widespread negative attitude toward its use. Spanglish continues to be used in Hispanic communities, however, and more study needs to be done to better determine its place in new generations.[30]

Several points will help us understand the issue of Spanglish. First, it is natural for most immigrants to blend their native language with English. The Norwegians, for example, changed many English words to fit their Norwegian syntax:

In order to "maeka ei levving" they had to scratch about for a "jabb" which often meant that they had to join a "kru" (crew) of some kind and work under a "bas." . . . Many Norwegians found work in the "lomberkemper." . . . If they could not afford to buy a farm they might "renta" and live as "rentarar," "leiga" and "lielending."[31]

Second, Spanglish is different from "code-switching," the switching from one language to another during a conversation. Many studies indicate that bilinguals tend to code-switch, though a bilingual will not switch when the other speaker is monolingual.[32]

Third, Spanglish does not destroy or abandon basic Spanish structure. Expressions like "está en el beisman" ("he is in the basement") and "el rufo está liqueando" ("the roof is leaking") indicate that Spanish structure still prevails.[33]

Fourth, Spanglish produces barriers between first- and second-generation Hispanics, largely because Spanglish is perceived as inferior to the Spanish language. When U.S.-born and raised Hispanics who primarily speak English visit Puerto Rico, Cuba or Mexico, they feel like outsiders because they do not speak Spanish like a native. In other Spanish-speaking situations, they feel ashamed when they are constantly told by others that they are speaking Spanish poorly. Their feelings of rejection and inferiority prompt an identity crisis.

"Spanglish" has been used by the dominant society to support the idea that minorities are "linguistically deficient" and/or "verbally deprived." From both sides, then, there is a rejection of the immigrant's language which will obviously have a serious impact on the individual's self-concept.[34]

Integration always takes the form of the dominant culture. It happens not only in Spanish culture, but in all immigrant cultures.

Note the following adaptations made by a number of immigrant groups:

| English | Norwegian-American |
| --- | --- |
| anyway | eunivei |
| fixes | fiksar |
| factory | fektri |
| makes | mekar |

| English | Dutch-American |
| --- | --- |
| trouble | troebel |
| to move | moeven |
| stores | storen |
| to drive | drivuen |

| English | Polish-American |
| --- | --- |
| truck | trok |
| street car | strytkara |
| job | dziab |
| payday | pedja |

| English | Finnish-American |
| --- | --- |
| store | stoori |
| teacher | titseri |
| baby | peipi |
| to clear | kliinaan |

| English | Italo-American |
| --- | --- |
| furniture | fornitura |
| nurse | nursa |
| to fix | fixare |
| trouble | trobolo |

| English | Spanglish |
| --- | --- |
| furniture | furnitura |

| | |
|---|---|
| nurse | norsa |
| to fix | fixear |
| trouble | trobol[35] |

"All these immigrant groups . . . 'make up' their own words by incorporating English words into the phonological and morpho-logical system of their respective languages."[36]

In Acosta-Belén's study of bilingual college students and their acceptance of Spanglish words, "67 percent of the 'Spanglish' words were considered acceptable by the students and 72 percent of the words were commonly used by them." On the other hand, "only 35 percent were able to provide the 'correct' Spanish equiv-alents."[37] Acosta-Belén concluded that children of first-generation parents are slowly but surely losing command of Spanish as it is spoken in their parents' home country.

Language is more than a legitimizer that installs and keeps you in a cultural identity. Language is also communication and enrich-ment. Determining one's ethnicity and commitment by language alone is extremely exclusivistic. Linguistic realities should never be used to exclude, remove or alienate others, especially those of similar cultural roots. Only when we begin to accept others, listen and learn from them with great interest, and allow ourselves to enter into each other's world will we be able to reverse the language limitations of the second and third generations.

## Conclusion
New beginnings are always filled with anxiety and fear. The Hispanic groups mentioned in this chapter provide a certain insight into working with not only the immigrants but also the American-born who are searching for their place of significance both in this country and in their own culture. All face enormous hardship in a society that still questions who is dominant and who is inferior. For the second generation—even more than the first—a profound identity crisis makes for additional suffering for children born to

Hispanic families who came to this country in search of a better life.

Some cultural groups in the U.S. believe they have the sole right to determine who comes into their communities and fills "their" jobs. They do not open their arms to newcomers and invite them to take hold of the American dream. Sadly, they see only themselves as having that privilege. It is as though they placed a stop sign in their neighborhoods declaring, "stay out" and "keep out."

A greater conflict exists when the church also closes its doors to new arrivals from Latin American countries. It is a great tragedy and offends our Lord, who stands with those who are oppressed.

# SECTION II

---

# Missiological/
# Ecclesiastical
# Issues

# Chapter 4

---

# Protestant-Roman Catholic Dialogue

A nyone who thinks he or she can grasp all present and future Hispanic missiological issues in North America is either courageous or foolish. The Latin American impact on this country will continue to grow indefinitely, providing many unforseen challenges. We are now living in a "global village," and in that "village" more than 90 percent of U.S. Hispanics live in the cities. This globalization-urbanization process must be recognized and applied to the church's present agenda.

Concentrations of the Third World in the United States are especially evident in urban areas. Blacks and Hispanics constitute close to or over 50 percent of the population of New York, Chicago, Atlanta, Detroit, Baltimore, Philadelphia, Cleveland and Los Angeles. . . . Three hundred thousand Salvadorans reside in Los Angeles.[1]

Immigration policy will invade the domestic-urban scene and, in particular, mission strategy and denominational attitudes for those who wish to be on the "cutting edge." How the U.S.-Latin American relationship affects the economic and political structures in Latin America will factor in to the way we do ministry in the barrios of North America.

The Hispanic population in the United States has swelled to 25.4 million, including the 3 million living in Puerto Rico. This growth, along with the increased democratization of the political process, has and will continue to strengthen Hispanic political clout, not only in the Southwest but also in the Northeast. Before long, this growing political power will, for instance, lead to nationwide policies on bilingual issues in education.[2] In comparison, twenty years ago Spanish-speaking children were placed in classes where only English was spoken and were disciplined if they spoke in Spanish, no matter what the reason.[3] Also, the increased Latinization of the U.S. by those with limited commitments to the "American Way" has prompted new thinking about present immigration policies. Appleby, in his volume *Missions Come Home to America,* indicates that 38 percent of our yearly immigration, not including refugees and undocumented, comes from Latin America.[4]

Another major concern is the dialogue between Protestants and Roman Catholics—often reviewed in missiological journals but rarely found as an ongoing praxis in the U.S.

The shift from Eurocentrism to what William Dyrness calls an *intercultural body* or a *theology of the people* is presenting a challenge to theological education in North America.[5] Goizueta highlights what he calls a "shift from a Eurocentric to a polycentric Christianity."[6] My point is that the Third World church must be viewed as more than a "church outside Europe."[7]

Globalization and its importance to the task of doing theology here in the United States will raise new tensions. Latin American theology can no longer be viewed as foreign or, as Deck notes, "exotic," but rather as significant to dominant theologies.[8] Here we need to face the difficulty of pluralism and its impact on North

American intellectuals. Will the Third World church and its offering of theology and missiology continue to be minimized? In our
seminaries, we will need to discuss the value not only of the Western
philosophical tradition, but also of sociology and anthropology as
tools in doing theology, recognizing that knowledge is an interpretation of reality.[9]

This section will present some of the missiological and theological issues facing the Hispanic community, but, as previously mentioned, it will only touch on a few of these issues.

## Protestant-Roman Catholic Dialogue

The following brief discussion will probably disappoint and frus-
trate many readers, because it does not go far enough in doing
justice to the issue. Yet I chose to make this subject my starting point
in order to express a sense of urgency. I hope that others who
recognize the need for a current evaluation of this dialogue will
develop the subject further.

As a Puerto Rican who emerged from the Roman Catholic
experience, I was instructed by my early biblical professors to stay
away from and be suspicious of the Roman Catholic church. I also
discovered that many of my Protestant brothers and sisters who
came from the Mexican-American milieu had a similar profound
dislike for Roman Catholic clergy. There are many reasons for this
attitude, from history to theology to tradition. But I believe we have
entered a new context of life and spirit in which we desire not to
compromise our basic beliefs but rather to enhance and affirm
them. In this chapter I touch on the Roman Catholic-Protestant
dialogue, while acknowledging the need for more interaction and
more research.

## Roman Catholic Heritage

Many, if not most, Hispanics would rather enter the doors of a
church than the halls of a university, or read the Bible than study
Puerto Ricanism. We would rather indulge in the miracles of the

93

Holy Spirit than take on political discussions. The church, particularly the Roman Catholic church, lies at the heart of Hispanic culture. Justo González reminds us, "The Spanish-American Roman Catholic church is part of the common background of all Hispanics—if not personally, then at least in our ancestry."[10] Growing up in New York City, I do not recall any non-Catholics in our community. Communities were not only segregated by ethnicity, they were also religiously polarized. To be Roman Catholic was to be authentically Christian. This has been true for all Hispanic groups. In fact, "It is frequently said that to be a Colombian is to be a Catholic."[11] We called our children Jesús and María to stress the importance of Christianity in our culture. Many desired their children to become priests, nuns or pastors. To be Protestant, I recall hearing, was to be white, rich and questionably Christian.

The church, both Roman Catholic and Protestant, is pivotal to the future of all generations of all U.S. Hispanic groups. It must learn to bridge the generational conflicts and address the unique needs and gifts of each group, especially the second and third generation. Much more than language adjustments are needed. We must take a deep look into the life and worldview of each generation.

The Roman Catholic church has always played an important role in meeting the needs of new immigrants coming to America, especially those from Catholic countries. However, historically, the Catholic church's ministry to immigrants on the national level[12] has been identified with the church of the middle and upper classes, leaving many Puerto Ricans, Mexicans and Central Americans feeling rejected.

> Mexican immigrants found little sympathy for their plight among Spanish-speaking elite. They were ignored and despised by the resident Spanish-speaking aristocracy, and likewise they received little or no help from the impoverished Roman Catholic church.[13]

Early Cuban immigrants may not have felt this way about the

Roman Catholic church in Florida, perhaps because many of them were well-established economically. In the years after the Cubans first arrived in 1962, the Catholic church in Miami doubled in size to more than 300,000.[14]

Many Hispanics in the U.S. also felt that the Catholic church didn't care about their culture because it rarely installed Hispanic priests and refused to make certain changes in worship traditions that would meet cultural and generational needs. In fact, the biggest obstacle to helping Latin Americans in their new journey has been the lack of Hispanic clergy. In Miami this was no problem, because many of the priests in Cuba had fled and joined the Miami archdiocese.[15]

Nominalism and decline in the Roman Catholic church in the U.S. can be traced in part to cultural and ethnic issues, as well as the role the Catholic church played in colonizing Latin America and the Caribbean.[16] But I would add that the Holy Spirit is at work. The renewal movement in the Roman Catholic church has not only brought new life, but it has also given room for lateral movement among Protestant charismatics. Both Roman Catholic and Protestant charismatic groups have a certain affinity with each other, and in some cases Roman Catholics have left their church to become leaders and indigenous pastors in the evangelical charismatic church. David Martin declares, "The more the Catholic church feels itself under pressure, the more it may become like its competitors."[17] Regardless of the reasons, this Roman Catholic nominalism opened further doors for Protestant contacts and affiliations.

Along these lines, Roberto Goizueta has addressed the issue of what he calls consumers of religions.[18] His argument is well taken:

> In the name of individual freedom, the individual has been loosed from preexistent ties to community and tradition, has become increasingly mobile both physically and psychologically, has been afforded the "freedom to choose," has, in the process, surrendered the very communal and traditional bonds (at least as a priori, constitutive dimensions) that have heretofore pro-

vided the necessary ground and frame of reference from which to choose, and has, therefore, been set psychologically adrift, a manipulable pawn in the hands of the dominant ideology and its purveyors.[19]

And so, this consumerism continues as we shop for the "right" church in our ecclesiastical shopping mall.

The question of the poor and their powerlessness in urban ghettos has brought a certain amount of discomfort to the Roman Catholic church. Within the Catholic church, the poor are pressuring it to become more visibly involved in justice issues. Even some priests who hold high positions in the church are echoing a concern for justice. Many of these leaders were selected not through the process of "nobility," but through the avenue permitted them as "grassroots" priests who climbed the ladder into the hierarchy. Now they are bringing the cry of the poor to the church.[20]

## Hispanic Protestants

Protestantism is not as well documented as Catholicism.

The initial Protestant movement sparked by missionary James Thomson brought a sense of spiritual liberation to many—freedom from Spain, the freedom of ordinary people to read and study the Bible on their own, and the freedom for all to lead and participate in worship. People realized they were able to speak to God and praise God without supervision. This, to me, was a radical departure.

Placing the Bible in the hands of the people and inviting them to examine it freely was a revolutionary act. Protestant worship, where people participated actively, was also an act of empowerment and liberation.[21]

The major manifestations of Protestantism in my community came from storefront churches in New York City. They were alive, energetic and an open door for the poor. The church of the poor in New York was Pentecostal and Baptist. Its leaders were from the

community and had no formal education. In Latin America the
case is similar.

> For all kinds of reasons, and with some exceptions, Latin Amer-
> ican Protestantism was in its origins, and to a great extent still is,
> a church of the poor.[22]

We are not so naive as to generalize about the church's commitment to the poor, however. Many mainline and independent
churches have embraced a different ideology. Economic expansion was extended further than government and political ambi-
tions. The historic churches climbed the wagon of success. It was a
time to improve life through church affiliation, a means for social
climbing.[23]

Both in Latin America and in the U.S., Hispanic Protestants show
great enthusiasm for preaching the gospel and building churches
in urban communities. Indeed, the Hispanic church is leading in
church growth and evangelism. Many of the Hispanic churches are
Pentecostal and charismatic. The independent charismatic movement, which David Barrett calls the *second wave*, is the fastest-growing segment in Christianity.[24] Interestingly, many church planters
and pastors find Hispanic communities in U.S. cities a natural place
to establish new ministries. These churches are monolingual and
at times monocultural (i.e., Cuban, Puerto Rican, Mexican, etc.)
here in North America. Those sent from the U.S. to Latin America
feel equally comfortable planting churches in the cities.

**Dialogue**

The one major influence both in Protestantism and Roman Catholicism is the significance of the Scriptures in the life of the Christian.
The reading and teaching of the Word of God has transformed
many lives. The influence of the charismatic movement in Protestant mainline churches and in the Catholic church provides an
avenue for fellowship and dialogue. But what should the content
of the dialogue be?

In various places and at several levels of the Protestant and

*97*

Catholic church, dialogue is going on. I do not know what the outcome will be. But I strongly believe that it must be continued, and that it can lead to much gain for the kingdom of God.

Historically, the Hispanic religious experience is steeped in Roman Catholicism. Reactions emanating from these roots have in some cases been devastating to Protestantism because they have set up barriers between Roman Catholics and Protestants and limited Protestant-Catholic cooperation. Yet most cities provide a natural environment for Protestants and Catholics to network and share experiences and resources. Both recognize the enormous needs of the people and face shortages of personnel, resources and encouragement. In Chicago I was called on by the Catholic church to participate in services pertaining to social problems such as the strike against drug dealing or the protest over gang violence. Often I was asked to officiate at a funeral of a gang member who was killed by a rival gang. So the urban areas in which Protestants and Catholics are already networking and supporting each other can provide a place for ongoing dialogue.

Seminaries are also interested in hearing positions on ecclesiastical and theological themes that will provide greater understanding of what Catholics and Protestants truly believe. For example, five seminaries in the Philadelphia area, four Protestant and one Roman Catholic, have come together to offer an elective which will allow students to dialogue on various themes. This offers great opportunity for getting to know faculty and students of both persuasions, as well as offering significant space for serious dialogue.

Recently in one of my classes, I invited a seminarian from St. Charles Borromeo Roman Catholic Seminary to share his experience and theological position. This particular student was rooted in conservative evangelical doctrine and had attended various evangelical Bible schools and seminaries. While attending one of these institutions, a dynamic conversion occurred that caused him to rethink his religious commitments. He decided to join what he saw as the only true church, the Roman Catholic church. When he visited my class, he zealously urged our reformed and evangelical students to return to their faith and to the early church. His evangelistic thrust sent a shock wave through our Protestant students, yet his call to unity and to the Catholic church could not be ignored. This is one example of how discussions are occurring in the academic and pastoral arenas. An honest commitment to this process will, I hope, break down resistance and hostility in both groups.

The foreword in González's *Mañana,* written by Virgilio P. Elizondo, is a moving statement by a Roman Catholic theologian who speaks from his heart about his love for his people and his church. Yet he is also balanced in his concern for honest dialogue.

> Yes, there is truly a new ecumenism in the common struggle for justice, but there is also a new ecumenism in the new knowledge that is emerging out of the common struggle. It is just beginning. It is not yet developed.[25]

A number of years ago, while I served in Chicago's Humboldt Park community, I had the privilege of meeting Sister Dominga Zapata, a missionary theologian from Puerto Rico. She was a wonderful example of the servant heart of Christ. One day in a combined celebration she had the opportunity to interact with some of the second-generation Hispanic leaders of our community. At the conclusion, after hearing her testimony and passion for the gospel, one of the leaders from an evangelical church said, "My, I didn't realize you were a Christian." She responded, "I also did not realize that you were a Christian."

Much more needs to be done to engage God's plan of unity in the midst of diversity. The dialogue between Roman Catholics and Protestants is transformational and missiological.

# Chapter 5

# The Poor
# and
# Justice

If "prosperity" has become a key concept of ministry for many dynamic, growing Hispanic churches, how shall we continue to be light in the most needy and oppressed communities? Given that many Hispanics, perhaps even the largest percentage, are Pentecostal or charismatic, their history begins with the poor.

Most of us classic Pentecostals came from the blue-collar, working-class group. And the thing that made Pentecostalism grow was that they took the Gospel to the poor. We must never forget our roots, regardless of how the Gospel has lifted us materially.[1] This connection between Pentecostals and the poor may be in question, as Grant Wacker notes. Pentecostalism is a spiritual movement which does not provide "consolation to the poor but confirmation to the successful."[2] Will the urban poor find refuge in the growing "prosperous" Hispanic church in the United States?

In spite of growth in the Hispanic community, oppression has not diminished. Racism is rampant in our communities, and the church must revisit the Scriptures in order to renew its commitment to the needy and marginalized people of the city. Psalm 12:5 tells us, " 'Because of the oppression of the weak and the groaning of the needy, I will now arise,' says the Lord. 'I will protect them from those who malign them.' "

As Villafañe states, "The minority church, the Hispanic church in the U.S.A., is the 'church of the poor.' "[3] This has long been true, and I do not see a major departure from this position, but I do become concerned that the church feels caught between its social life and ministry to the poor. Because of a variety of circumstances, ministry among the urban poor may be less likely in the coming decade.

Hispanics are an important dimension of the charismatic movement in the U.S. In 1973, David Wilkerson voiced his concern that "tongues have moved uptown."[4] Whatever we may think of this shift, it has occurred, and among those left behind are many Hispanic communities that continue to struggle with socioeconomic limitations and oppression. I find it striking that leaders of groups such as Victory Outreach and Teen Challenge speak of how they work in the hardest and most difficult communities, giving the clear impression that to work in the city takes a "specialty group" or requires people who have come out of a rough and difficult life. This approach only makes it more credible to move away. I can hear my brothers and sisters saying, "We must leave this crime-infested community before we become contaminated." Because of economic and educational resources, we now have alternatives and options we never had before. We may not realize it, but theology stands at the forefront of this issue.

## Commitment to the Poor

We must remember that "prosperity gospel" theology does not limit itself to Pentecostal or charismatic churches. Many denominations are embracing this theology, though its manifestations vary. It breeds apathy and a relocation mentality among those in oppressed and powerless communities. "We are all going to the promised land," which to more and more people means up and out of the inner city.

A wonderful testimony by Eldin Villafañe emphasized one man's firm commitment to John 3:16 Church in New York City.

Rev. Tañon never forgot his roots among the poor and disinherited. While other pastors and churches sought "greener" pastures, he stood firm. On many occasions as the church grew in numbers and economic resources, many wanted to move out of the "ghetto"—only to be reminded and challenged by Rev. Tañon that there in the dirty and dark streets of Prospect and Westchester Avenues in the Bronx God wanted them to shine like a lighthouse to offer a beacon to the shipwrecked.[5]

God may be asking for a similar commitment from second- and third-generation Hispanics: to return to the communities they had always dreamed of leaving. It will be difficult, perhaps impossible, to move back voluntarily. But if some of us don't return, our judgment of the Anglo community for leaving the inner city when times got tough and the neighbors changed color and lifestyle may haunt us in the future.

God's will must be our criterion for going or staying. The universal mandate of the Word of God must touch all cultures and socioeconomic classes. Some missions experts such as Peter Wagner continue to propagate the message that God's call is for "some only":

The Christian community, rightly so, has been developing a growing compassion for the poor, the oppressed, the minorities, the homeless, and the handicapped. God loves these people and desires that churches be planted among them. But He obviously does not call everyone to do it.[6]

I must disagree with Wagner here. God's calling to minister to the urban poor applies to all of us. Viv Grigg notes,

Did he not say, "As the Father has sent me, I sending you" (Jn 20:21)? And did not his first declaration of his own great commission tell us:

> The Spirit of the Lord is on me, because he has anointed me to preach good news to the poor. He has sent me to proclaim freedom for the prisoners and recovery of sight for the blind, to release the oppressed, to proclaim the year of the Lord's favor (Lk 4:18-19)?[7]

Grigg goes on to say that missiological analysis has led to several conclusions. First is that "urban is the direction of history." Second, "the poor are the direction of responsiveness. This is true in Jesus' teaching and in missions' history as well as in sociological analysis."[8]

The key issue for the poor is not their lack of material well-being; it is their powerlessness and their inability to determine their own destiny. The Lord tells us,

> With my mouth I will greatly extol the LORD;
>
> in the great throng I will praise him.
>
> For he stands at the right hand of the needy one,
>
> to save his life from those who condemn him. (Ps 109:30-31)

Children are dying because of poverty. Within the last year more than 130 million children have died from preventable poverty conditions.[9]

## Americanization

The American process has without a doubt infiltrated the interpretation of the gospel. In many communities people have *over-contextualized* the gospel out of concern for the whole person to the point that they have compromised the whole gospel. Yet I am also encouraged by some second-generation leaders in my city who are attacking the evils of society and providing proper resources to relieve and empower the powerless.

My desire is to see Christians relocate into urban areas wherever we have departed from the needy—especially Hispanic and African-American communities. On the other hand, I would like to see those Christians already living in these areas stay put, as difficult as that may seem. It is Christ who sustains us and maintains our destiny. The church that was located in the city but has migrated to better surroundings may need to review its vows toward the community and the poor.

> Do not deprive the alien or the fatherless of justice, or take the cloak of the widow as a pledge. Remember that you were slaves in Egypt and the LORD your God redeemed you from there. That is why I command you to do this. (Deut 24:17-18)

I am deeply concerned about the Hispanic church and its increasing departure not only from the city but also from the poor. If the church approaches the issue with sociological eyes, it may want to find greener pastures to avoid being swallowed up by the rapid growth and social deterioration. If it views the reality of urban density with theological eyes without the social interaction, it may want to find a place of "refuge" so that unrighteousness may not win over righteousness. The church must not view the church as an end in itself, nor must it allow its mission to become marginalized. Israel fell into that trap and saw herself as the center and end of life rather than the means to mission and exaltation of the God of history.[10]

Imagine this scenario. Many of our people have come from shantytowns—poor barrios in Latin America—have moved to U.S. cities and have become poor in a foreign context. In some ways they are poorer than before, because they now have to deal with clear lines of exclusion and racial segregation on all levels of life. When Hispanics realize they are unwanted, they experience one of the most profound stages of poverty. They fight and scrape to make a new life, the American way of life featured in TV commercials. The gospel of Christ becomes a means to a new life and new mission. Their lifestyle changes, and they receive blessing upon blessing. They have a new motivation for success and for acquiring the things often out of reach of majority Americans.

As the scenario continues, the church focuses on those who are experiencing this new life and incorporates new leaders into its ministry. Before long, pastors begin to talk about how sensible and socially responsible it is for the church to move outside the community. The church, eager to follow its leaders' example, embraces the plan and the exodus begins. The community will either stay the same, as it often does, or it may experience a greater social disaster and spiritual vacuum than before: no salt or light except on Wednesdays and Sundays, no biblical incarnation—Christians living in and being a part of the community—to tell the old story of Christ and his redemption. Now the church has become the community which has truly "made it" for the first time. Whether the church stays or comes back, the community will continue to need God.

Orlando Costas provides a note of conviction when he says,

Jesus died outside the gate, and in so doing changed the place of salvation and clarified the meaning of mission. No longer can I see God's saving grace as an individual benefit, a privileged possession, or a religious whitewash that enables me to feel good and continue to live the old way because my bad conscience has been soothed and my guilt feelings washed away. On the contrary, because salvation is to be found in the crucified Son of God who died outside the gate of the religious compound, to be saved by faith in him is to experience a radical transformation that makes me a "debtor" to the world (Rom 1:14) and calls me forth to share in his suffering by serving, especially, its lowest representatives: the poor, the powerless, and the oppressed.[11]

Are we asking too much? We must return to our biblical roots. We have always understood the spiritual realm of life, and now as Christians, we know that our weapons are not carnal but spiritual.

We must not view our calling to serve among the poor for Christ and his kingdom as a means of gaining new status or respect in the American context. Rather, our job in the church is to reinvent the biblical wheel of justice and righteousness *in the milieu of the impoverished.* As Dominga Zapata would say, we must do theology *desde el pueblo y para el pueblo,* that is, "*from* the community and *for* the community."

The Hispanic evangelical church has always assumed that its commitment was more spiritual than social and that the social transformation was incidental, not primary. Yet what has happened among Hispanic Christians is that the social has become a goal of the Christian life—numerical growth, preachers with national and international status, networking with evangelical bigwigs, aiming to be the Hispanic Bill Cosbys of our society.

All of this shows that we are imposing the values of the world on our Christian faith. Like our Euro-American brothers and sisters, we too have assumed that the "good" aspect of being an American is the Christian part, and that becoming a part of Middle America is to be more Christian. It is nothing less than a scheme of Satan, and in North America it shows no sign of letting up.

If the church does not maintain a visible witness in the city, spiritism, Islam and Jehovah's Witnesses will. We need the kind of revival that will move us toward the biblical image of the servant Christ—the Christ who voluntarily displaced himself to live and identify with the have-nots of the world.

# Chapter 6

# Reconciliation

The Great Commission directs us toward crosscultural and incarnational ministries. What will we do about communities in transition, in which our new neighbors speak different languages, look different from us and act in ways unfamiliar to Hispanics? Will the African-American, Asian or Anglo community be excluded from hearing the gospel because we insist on speaking only Spanish in our local churches?

The process of reconciliation must include a new mission—that of dialogue between African-Americans and Hispanics. Most often we have focused on the alienation between the Anglo community and the Hispanics living nearby in the city. But little has been said about the need for reconciliation between Hispanics and people of color. The assumption is that the Hispanic community harbors no biases or racist attitudes, especially in regard to African-Americans. Unfortunately, this information is incorrect and misleading.

For example, many believe that the island of Puerto Rico has no racial prejudice. Samuel Betances, a professor at Northeastern University in Chicago, disagrees. "To suggest that Puerto Rico is free of race prejudice is to ignore reality,"[1] he writes. Much of this ignorance comes from not recognizing the historical impact of old Iberian slave laws. Betances goes on to say that "historical evidence, past and present, indicates the presence of violence and race prejudice in Puerto Rico."[2] In short, my pressing concern is the issue of reconciliation, particularly between African-Americans and Hispanics.

In the city we are usually living shoulder to shoulder, and the existing system has pitted us against each other. Consider the following from an article by Linda Chavez:

> For more than a quarter century, blacks and Hispanics have been seen as allies in the civil rights struggle. No longer. Hispanics, who are quickly overtaking blacks as the nation's largest minority group, are furious that blacks treat civil rights as their private domain.[3]

This kind of attitude may cause two groups who have previously been aligned in matters of justice to mistrust and exclude each other. She goes on to say,

> Hispanic leaders want to redefine the civil rights agenda to include immigration reform and to increase Hispanic political power, even if it means defeating black candidates.[4]

The issue of employment for African-Americans drives a wedge into this discussion. Will immigrants get jobs that are appropriate for African-Americans? If so, then the fight against Hispanics and other non-English-speaking groups will continue.

> Hazel Dukes, president of the NAACP's national board of directors, charged that non-English-speaking immigrants are getting jobs that should go to blacks.[5]

In order to reach the city, we must learn the importance of working together with the African-American community. In some cases we need to reconcile differences that have kept both communities separate. We must develop and implement a partnership in order to approach the societal and spiritual issues that threaten our youth and families.

The very strength of monocultural development can also be our weakness. The cultural and socioeconomic pluralism in the U.S. has made it extremely difficult for ethnic groups to develop significant relationships with each other. It occurs rarely in society and even less in the evangelical church. The same penetrating question asked of our Anglo brothers and sisters since the civil rights movement can be asked of the Hispanic church in North America: How shall we reconcile differences and find wholeness and partnership in ministry with the African-American church? We usually occupy the same urban turf and face the same societal problems. A united front will be extremely important to the future of our people in the city.

In missiological terms, how shall we minister together and to each other in this crosscultural context? Are the limitations a matter of linguistic ability? Should the uniqueness of our cultures build walls of separation because we prefer certain traditions and styles of worship? Is it a matter of racial and ethnic prejudice? Both biblical practices and principles make it clear that we in the church are called to move beyond the parameters of our comfort/culture zone. Paul reminds the church of Ephesus that Christ is our peace, that he destroyed both religious and cultural barriers (Eph 2:14-22). We must broaden our evangelistic borders and begin this crucial process of dialogue and reconciliation with our African-American brothers and sisters.

## Media Manipulation
Some of the alienation between Hispanics and African-Americans has stemmed from media reports that seem to pit the various ethnic groups against each other in a great competition. For example, the April 9, 1990, issue of *Time* magazine was subtitled, "What will the U.S. be like when whites are no longer the majority? America's changing colors."

Already 1 American in 4 defines himself or herself as Hispanic or nonwhite. If current trends in immigration and birth rates persist, the Hispanic population will have further increased an estimated 21%, the Asian presence about 22%, blacks almost 12% and whites a little more than 2% by the end of the 20th century.[6]

How does that grab you? It feels uncomfortable. I am, and have been, suspicious of this data and its underlying purpose. An African-American friend at Princeton said, "I can't put my finger on it, but it does not feel good."

Justo González affirms my discomfort:

Some naive Hispanics rejoice in that finally attention is being paid to them. But others realize that this is simply another instance of playing one minority against the other, and that the articles . . . to be read by Afro-Americans and other minorities [will say], "watch out, here come the Hispanics."[7]

González speaks for many of us. He also says,

And let us not deceive ourselves into believing that the games mentioned above are played only in "secular" society. In churches, church agencies, church colleges, and seminaries, the same games are played. A portion of the budget, a number of positions, or a few courses in a curriculum are reserved for "minority concerns," and then we are encouraged to fight it out, as if our struggle were against one another and not against the basic injustices of the present order.[8]

## Steps Toward Reconciliation

What can be done to bring about reconciliation between African-Americans and Hispanics? There are many issues that confront both communities, such as poverty, single mothers, substance abuse and AIDS. Hispanics and African-Americans have unemployment rates more than twice as high as those of Anglos. Both communities live in the city and have limited representation in local government. Also, most urban churches are African-American or Hispanic. If these local churches formed a partnership to pursue justice and edification, it would be a major step toward reconciliation.

Keeping two considerations in mind will enhance this dialogue. First, we must recognize that too often our actions, attitudes and ecclesiastical behavior have been exclusive, motivated by ethnocentrism and prejudices. We need to feel remorse over the sins we have committed against each other. Orlando Costas says, "Sin, then, is every unjust act—every lack of consideration for the well-being of one's neighbor, every insult to human dignity, every act of violence done by one to someone else."[9]

Recognizing that sin means injustice, Costas reminds us that the gospel works toward justification and liberation[10] but must first be ignited by hearts of repentance. He notes that repentance is first turning from idols, injustice and selfishness and then unconditional commitment to the gospel.[11]

Second, we must recognize our need for each other. The apostle Paul writes, "The eye cannot say to the hand, 'I don't need you!'" (1 Cor 12:21). The willingness to go beyond our cultural zone and approach each other with an attitude of humility and openness will produce partners in the city. This relationship building must be ongoing and personal. As it progresses, local churches can get involved. This is often done by combined worship. It is rare to see Hispanic and African-American churches coming together for a joint worship service, but several churches in New York City and Chicago are enjoying this kind of fellowship. Ongoing dialogue between leaders and congregations should lead to prayer, strategizing, and a united effort to have an impact on the city for Jesus Christ.

## Role of the Pastor

Pastors are in a key position to initiate the reconciliation process by getting to know other pastors of different ethnic backgrounds. Too often we spend time only with other Hispanic pastors, while overlooking the pastor of the African-American church around the corner. And yet the following Sunday morning we will call our congregation to live in harmony and peace with our neighbors. What we are really doing is urging our people to ignore our neighbors, especially if they are different from us. It is so true that we allow our comfort zone to determine our mission and our associations. The gospel calls us to unity in diversity. If pastors would be willing to reach out and pray with others of diverse backgrounds, I believe we would take a giant step toward reconciliation. Such a deliberate move can lead to honest conversation that focuses on bringing unity to the body of Christ. Attitudes that have built up over generations would be challenged and, I hope, brought to repentance.

If the pastors begin to meet regularly, the church leaders and congregations will follow in their footsteps, usually by organizing a combined worship service. This is an important start, but we must also pursue other ways of coming together. The ministry of reconciliation in the community is best done by those committed to doing reconciliation in the body of Christ. When African-Americans come together with Hispanics to share the transforming gospel, the unity and love empowers their evangelism. Ministries of mercy, where food and clothing are distributed in a combined effort, are a true sign of the kingdom of heaven. Unless the African-American and Hispanic church come together and create a united front, the injustice that occurs in our communities will remain too strong. We must speak out for justice as one voice.

**New Mission Directives**
As we heed the crosscultural imperative of missions, we will not only enhance the work of the kingdom in the community, but will also enrich each local congregation. The growth of the Hispanic population in the United States should challenge the church to consider new frontiers for mission. The emerging leaders within the Hispanic church must not be ignored, but instead invited into a fellowship of leaders who are serious about participating in God's mission to the world. Mission must be discussed with second- and

third-generation Hispanics, who have much insight into the future of the urban church. The experience and sociological development of this younger, more aggressive segment of the Hispanic church will be an important guide in the years ahead. First-generation Christians, too, are extremely important to the growth of our youth. Not knowing where we have come from is dangerous and hampers our ability to understand who we are. The language of our parents will forever be a part of our historical and cultural awareness. Love for each other must characterize our conversation and our outreach. To even consider which generation is superior or inferior will undoubtedly hinder the growth and advancement of the Hispanic church.

The Hispanic church in the U.S. has had an enormous and profound impact on the Latin American and North American world, yet little has been written about it. Our young people must celebrate the faith and achievements of our fathers and mothers in God's mission. This base of awareness and history will empower the new generation to develop healthy and profound concerns for God's work in liberation throughout the world. The interaction between the monolingual Hispanic church and the emerging young Hispanic leaders must be encouraged in order to pursue missions as a means of liberation rather than domestication.

A vibrant and growing Hispanic and African-American church can be found in the central cities of the U.S. The Christ of the city was declared by Luke: "For today in the city of David there has been born for you a Savior, who is Christ the Lord" (Lk 2:11 NASB). This one sent by God to redeem the world still dwells in the city among his people. The church is the redeemed, redeeming the city unto Christ. If it is clear that the African-American and Hispanic communities have a common problem, it is just as vivid that we have a common solution and future. We must form a partnership in our world of urban ministry. Our parameters must grow beyond the limited comfort zones of culture and tradition and extend to all our neighbors and neighborhoods.

# Chapter 7

# Ecclesiastical Structure

The emerging leadership in the Hispanic church will be distinctively different than the existing leadership. Why? Because the gap between second-generation and first-generation Hispanics is more complicated and profound than the normal generation gap. Within the Hispanic church, members are suspicious of those who alter cultural values or depart from cultural distinctives, thus forming a new cultural expression. The church must be ready to incorporate and advance with the challenge of the second-generation population. Rather than drive away many young people who could be potential leaders of the church and significant resources for God's kingdom, the church should build ministry models that maximize the fullness of the body. Several models can be explored.

## Model 1: Growing Alongside

This approach provides a certain amount of autonomy for second-generation leaders. They can develop their model of ministry without departing from the local church. They meet simultaneously with the Hispanic monolingual church. They prepare their own worship and Sunday school with the focus of meeting the needs of the second and third generation. They will accommodate both the Spanish and English languages and integrate the urban culture within the Hispanic-American dynamic. This model will not promote a separate church, but rather a part of the existing church that is trying to meet the needs of the emerging generation. Therefore, there will only be one governing board and, if at all possible, one facility and one mission statement broad enough to include the generational philosophy of ministry. This "alongside" ministry will deliberately conduct its other activities in tandem with the monolingual church to enhance relationships and display unity in the midst of diversity.

**Model 1 Diagram**

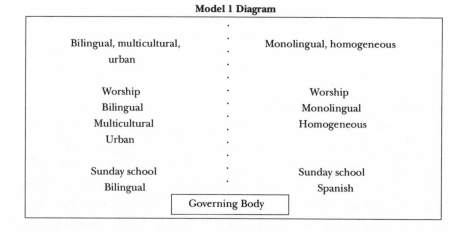

| Bilingual, multicultural, urban | Monolingual, homogeneous |
|---|---|
| Worship | Worship |
| Bilingual | Monolingual |
| Multicultural | Homogeneous |
| Urban | |
| Sunday school | Sunday school |
| Bilingual | Spanish |

Governing Body

## Model 2: Growing Within

This approach can be effective in churches with more than one language group. It is often implemented in Hispanic churches that are keenly aware of the need to minister to the second generation. Under this model, the church has one service and one Sunday school, but conducts these and all of its ministries in both English and Spanish. The service would use English and Spanish songs, and translate the message in summary form into either one of the languages. Usually Spanish is translated to English, either during or at the end of the message. This model has one governing body and is willing to include second-generation leaders on the board. The major Hispanic cultural tradition will dominate, and Spanish will be spoken more than 75 percent of the time. Culturally, the church will be Hispanic (more specifically, Mexican-American, Puerto Rican, Cuban, etc.) with linguistic adjustments only. It is crucial that certain activities and events be guided and developed by the second and third generations, ensuring that their needs are being met in a way that enriches and broadens their understanding of the first generation.

**Model 2 Diagram**

| Bilingual Service |
| One |
| Worship |
| Sunday school |
| Governing Body |

## Model 3: Growing Without

This model promotes the planting of a new church that will eventually disengage from the mother church. The second- and third-generation Hispanic Christians will be permitted to embark on a church-planting mission that may demand relocation. The existing church realizes its limitations and does not stand in the way of establishing a second-generation, bilingual, multiethnic church. Being mission-centered, the mother church sees its community as a mission field and is motivated to give away its best for the sake of the gospel. The new ministry will have its own leadership and governing board and will be self-supporting. It may or may not have combined services or mutual ministries. Again, the basic thrust will be to establish a new work. The mother church will continue to be a resource as long as the new church deems it necessary.

**Model 3 Diagram**

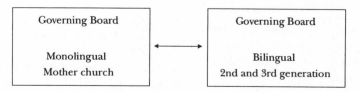

## Model 4: Growing Through House Churches

One way to accomplish model 3 is through small groups and house churches. This particular model focuses on developing a new ministry in the multiethnic urban context. This is a deliberate and missiological activity. It will be led by a second-generation urban Hispanic leader with a vision for the city and its pluralism. The leadership team will probably be multiethnic and urban. The central driving force of this work is mission—in particular, establishing new ministries. The model does not depend on leadership alone but rather incorporates the whole church in the missiological movement. It may come out of a traditional, monolingual Hispanic church, or it may arise from within an Anglo church that is homogeneous but desires to be involved in urban mission and church planting.

Spirit and Truth Fellowship church in Chicago used this approach and developed the following model description.

**Model 4 Diagram**

*Phase 1*

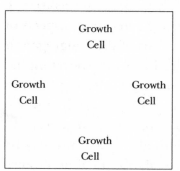

Characteristics:
1. Elders in charge
2. The church learning to be the bride of Christ in context
   a. Word taught and applied
   b. Worship
   c. Mobilization of believers: discipleship
   d. Multiplication: evangelism
3. Leadership in training: recognizing and developing leaders
4. Development of relationship: covenant

*Phase 2*

| | |
|---|---|
| Community<br><br>House<br>Church | Community<br><br>House<br>Church |
| House<br>Church<br><br>Community | House<br>Church<br><br>Community |

Characteristics:
1. House church leaders in charge and supervised by elders
2. The church becoming the church in context
3. House church has full responsibility of ministry in its location
4. Accountability and strategy
5. Development of pastors in context

*Phase 3*

| | |
|---|---|
| Church<br>in<br>Location | Church<br>in<br>Location |
| Church<br>in<br>Location | Church<br>in<br>Location |

Characteristics:
1. New elders and leaders pastoring
2. Original elders teaching, pastoring and establishing new ministry
3. The churches get together for celebrations and common ministries
4. Biblical autonomy: called to be together and to love one another
5. The church reproduces the process[1]

## Model 5: Growing into (Assimilation)

This approach emphasizes one church, one style and one language. Everyone adjusts and learns the traditions and language, and some help is given to those who are having difficulty. Most monolingual churches do not normally provide this assistance because they *assume* everyone will learn the necessary aspects of the ministry and culture. Often no analysis of the congregation is done to determine if the church has been incorporating the second and third generation into its ministry or losing them to other congregations. The model on page 122, carefully applied, can reduce the risk of losing bilingual, urban, second-generation people. However, it will lack crosscultural impact and may be vulnerable to apathy and declining attendance if cultural transitions occur in the community.

**Model 5 Diagram**

| Monolingual, homogeneous |
|---|
| One Board |
| One Worship |
| One Sunday School |

## Church Analysis

In my involvement as a consultant to local churches, I have discovered that the first and most important step to effective ministry is an informal analysis of the congregation. Trends in biological growth, percentage of youth in the community, and the number of young single parents will affect a church's plan for incorporation and growth over the next ten years. Discussing the results of this analysis can spur the leadership to develop a contextual model of ministry that will enhance the church and make a significant impact on the community.

On the other hand, the analysis may show that many of the young, second- and third-generation people have invested little in the church. After high school they may have stopped attending or may have become sporadic in their participation in church life. Information such as this will assist in bringing about change.

Planning and analysis are too often ignored in preference to the "movement" of the Holy Spirit. Analysis gives us insights not easily discovered with a casual look. It allows the church to form certain goals and evaluations to guide and direct the process. Of course, too much emphasis on analysis can certainly minimize the spontaneous movement of the Spirit by making the task seem too complicated and impossible.

Yet a strategy must be implemented. And it should have enough flexibility to allow for changes in the process.

There must also be an evaluation of the process itself, along with serious study of the Scriptures, to assure the church that it is avoiding syncretistic practices and accurately applying the precepts of the Word of God. Silva speaks of this caution:

> To interpret the biblical text (or any other text, for that matter) involves a *contextual shift*. Even when I seek merely to express what Paul meant, for example, I am constrained to do so in *my* situation: with English rather than Greek, with modern rather than ancient idioms, with Western nuances rather than Middle Eastern thought forms. In other words, all forms of interpretation necessarily include a measure of *contextualization*. This point is a little frightening because it appears to relativize Scripture.[2]

Prayer and more prayer should be the agenda of the church throughout all phases of analysis—prayer that is formed by a heart for the enhancement of God's kingdom in the world. Prayer has always been one of the greatest unifying factors in the Hispanic church, especially when motivated by mission.

## Obstacles to Change

Two things stand in the way of the Hispanic church's efforts to overcome the status quo. One is the lack of understanding of and confidence in the social sciences, particularly in the sociology of the church. This limits a church's ability to view the generational phenomena and determine how to respond. Culture will not be the same yesterday, today and forever. Second- and third-generation Hispanics have roots and wings. They are rooted in a Hispanic experience where their parents speak Spanish and review their culture through oral tradition. Their community (most live in a Hispanic community) also pulsates with the Hispanic experience. Music blasts from the stores; the aroma of food fills the streets. Their roots are deeper than most would imagine. But at the same time, for some, their wings are carrying them toward a changing society. Rap has joined the repertoire; hair styles and clothing mix African-American and Hispanic influences. The language continues to change as new words are added to the second- and third-generation vocabulary. The vision is different; hardships are as complicated and profound as ever and, in my opinion, much more

*123*

devastating. Change is the only unchanging phenomenon, but the change in the Hispanic community is more intense and radical than ever before.

The other obstacle is the lack of commitment to spreading the gospel no matter what the cost to cultural preservation. In other words, mission rather than cultural maintenance must be our highest priority. We must be willing to reach out to others who are different from us, recognizing that we live in a pluralistic, urban society that needs to be introduced to the Savior.

## Contextualization

For the Hispanic church, contextualization involves several elements. First is the willingness of heart to tackle the challenge. The openness to change or to expansion of one's tradition over against the mission of God in the world is an important initial step. Without this attitude the chances of success will be minimal.

The second element to contextualizing the church is the use of second- and third-generation Hispanics. Without their input and serious involvement, we may be going down the wrong street. This group needs to be part of the process from start to finish. These young people have a sense of direction as to outreach and ministries that will speak to their generation. Their hearts are more in tune with the emerging group of Hispanics who will eventually find growth and nurturing in this new milieu.

The third element is the involvement of the whole congregation. The church must be informed of the process and challenged to see the missiological importance. The church's involvement will provide for a healthy future. To ignore the congregation could build walls that would be impossible to overcome.

The fourth element to contextualizing the Hispanic church within the second generation is the concern for an integral theology, a theology that does not separate the soul from the body or the church from society. An evangelistic event must minister to people of "flesh and bone," conditioned by their time and space.[3]

Mission and theology must have meaning to a community. Evangelization is a social event, an act of genuine concern for people who find themselves in the same situation, people who need bread.[4] Our emerging leaders in the Hispanic community need further understanding of how to do theology in the hurting communities they come from. "How will God take care of our problems?" they ask. As René Padilla would say, contextualization is the act of being faithful to the Word of God and to the present social and historical situation one is serving. This is the constant task of the church in a changing and demanding world.

# SECTION III

---

## Leadership
## Training
## and
## Education

# Chapter 8

---

# Issues in
# Leadership
# Training

T he task of training and educating our emerging Hispanic leaders is a major issue for the church nationally. Sadly, our evangelical colleges have made hardly any effort to include the Hispanic-American. "Statistics for Fall 1983 showed that, on average, minority students (African-American, Hispanic-American, Asian-American, and Native American), represented 7.2 percent of total enrollment in CCC [Christian College Coalition] schools."[1] Further, Justo González stated in his volume *The Theological Education of Hispanics* that "the Association of Theological Schools barely touches the edge of the great number of Hispanics engaged in the ministry of word and sacrament—not to say anything of the even larger number of those involved in other forms of ministry."[2] How will the church equip the emerging second- and third-generation Hispanic leaders? These men and women are less conservative, usually urban, and often have bilingual, bicultural abilities, with English at times being the preferred language outside the home.

In order to provide a wide range of perspectives on how to approach the issue of second-generation emerging leadership, I spoke with six Hispanic leaders from across the country: Dr. Benjamin Alicea, the Reverend Luis Cortés, Dr. Isaac Canales, Dr. Alvaro Nieves, the Reverend Josue Abreu and the Reverend H. O. Espinoza. Two of these leaders are first-generation, and four are second-generation Hispanics. What follows are summaries of our conversations.

### Dr. Benjamin Alicea
### New York Puerto Rican (Reformed Church in America)

Alicea indicated that language is a primary concern for the development of the second generation. The Hispanic church in New York City has a perceived need to use Spanish. It tends to deny that the second and third generations use Spanish less comfortably and less easily than the first-generation members who control the church. This denial has led to the creation of a whole new genre of church—the English-speaking congregation heavily populated by Hispanics who were trained, prepared and grounded in the faith in a Spanish-speaking congregation but then transferred because they felt more comfortable speaking English. Unfortunately, the main beneficiary of this phenomenon is not the Hispanic church, but rather "superchurches" pastored by Anglos that may have sixty percent Hispanic membership. Many of the key lay leaders in these churches are Hispanic, yet the churches retain Anglo pastors and an entirely English-speaking format.

Alicea described two models as attempts by Hispanic churches to meet the needs of the second generation. The first was a very large Spanish-speaking congregation which started an English department. The English department grew dramatically, but eventually broke away from the Spanish congregation. The problem, as Alicea sees it, was that a dynamic, monolingual, monocultural

American led the English department. Though it began as an attempt to meet the needs of second-generation Hispanics, it fell into the "superchurch" mold.

The second model has been much more promising. A Hispanic bilingual and bicultural leader began a ministry in English with some Spanish. He worked with predominantly third-generation Hispanics and recognized their need to be comfortable in English but also their desire for certain parts of the service to be in Spanish. This church has actually moved in the opposite direction of most Hispanic churches: It is now trying to cultivate a separate Spanish-speaking congregation. Since the pastor understands the needs of both generations, works comfortably with both groups and can hold services in both languages, his ministry will probably succeed.

There are several different leadership-training avenues in New York City. Alicea indicates that mentoring is very effective. In this process, pastors take under their wing young men and women in whom they see a gift for ministry. Usually these are young people who exhibit abilities in the youth group. Little by little the pastor gives them counsel and responsibility. First the young people use their gifts outside the youth group (e.g., leading a song service or teaching Sunday school); then they receive additional responsibilities designed to stretch them. If they want to preach, they are often assigned to speak in street meetings—which challenge them to keep their message simple and to overcome their fear before groups.

Various formal educational opportunities are also available. During the last three years, between 4,000 and 5,000 students have studied at the many Bible institutes throughout the city. Lay leaders and potential ministerial leaders often attend these schools right after high school. Others go to college first (in the city or elsewhere) and then attend New York Theological Seminary. Currently there are fifty to one hundred potential leaders attending college and just under fifty enrolled in either the M.Div. or M.P.S. (Master of Professional Studies) programs at NYTS.

Alicea identified one other method of development—somewhat dangerous—which he calls the "jump in and swim" method. A gifted young person who has already completed work at a Bible institute is assigned to lead a small mission work somewhere in the city—perhaps three families meeting in a home or a storefront. The young leader receives very little training or support, but because of his or her gifts, manages to "wing it" and get the job done. The little group grows from a home to a storefront to renting a mainline Protestant church building. Eventually they may buy a church facility or convert a purchased garage or warehouse into a church. The process takes five to ten years. But some of these leaders burn out. And all of them pay a big price because family and personal goals must often be compromised in order to meet the church goals. Basically, these young leaders learn by making mistakes.

### The Reverend Luis Cortés
### Philadelphia Puerto Rican (American Baptist Convention)

Cortés sees the training of second-generation emerging leaders in Philadelphia as an informal process. He indicates that most of the key leaders have arisen naturally from within church ranks. As a church becomes involved in ministry, it recognizes potential leaders by their interest and involvement.

Since most of the Philadelphia Hispanic pastors are young—not only in age but also in spirit—they maintain good rapport with the emerging leaders and serve as excellent role models. Most of them disciple young Christians with a goal of strengthening the laity and reducing the distinction between pastoral and lay leadership. Unfortunately, the pastors do not have time to disciple as many as they would like. They would love to work with a group of twenty young people in order to glean ten committed potential leaders, but usually they only disciple one or two. Those who respond to a call to do lay ministry or go into professional ministry get the attention, but many more leaders are needed.

Cortés described the actual process of training as "learning as you go and do." Pastors take the young leaders with them and give them responsibilities and supervision. There is some personal counseling involved, but it is not intensive. Most of the learning occurs in the course of being together. It is not really planned, but happens as a response to ministry needs. Debriefing times help to bring home important lessons and principles.

The language issue is also important. The second generation wants a service primarily in English, yet they also need to retain some Spanish language and traditions in the services. It is important that the church allow these young people to have pride in their own identity—in who God created them to be.

Though there has been no intentional recruitment of leaders in the past, Hispanic clergy in the Philadelphia area are beginning to organize youth rallies, one goal of which will be to challenge and call young people to discipleship and ministry.

**Dr. Isaac Canales**
**California Mexican-American (Assembly of God)**
According to Canales, the first principle of developing second-generation Hispanic leaders is making sure they have a strong Christ-centered experience ("seek first the kingdom of God"). They need a sound base, an absolute, from which they can judge a society fraught with relativism. That strong center is the lordship of Jesus Christ. They must be able to judge other points of view from a strong Christian perspective and be able to dialogue without compromise.

A second principle is to take seriously the differences in language between the first and second generation; in other words, become bilingual. When the second generation loses the Spanish language, it cannot relate to the first generation. To avoid this, emerging second-generation leaders should learn to be bilingual so they can build a bridge between the first and third generations. Each generation tends to grow further away from its native language—its biggest cultural tie with the first generation. So leaders need to be proficient in both Spanish and English.

Second-generation leaders must be taught what it means to be world Christians, to understand how not one but many Hispanic cultures operate in the cities of North America. If leaders stay provincial, holding on to their own mother culture and excluding other Hispanic cultures, their effectiveness will be seriously limited. For example, Puerto Ricans should be able to understand and get along with Salvadorans, Mexicans, Cubans and so on. It requires the willingness to eat their food, speak their dialects, take their issues to heart. This is difficult for some second-generation leaders because they are often trying to get back to their own cultural roots. They must be careful not to go so deeply into their own Hispanic culture that they exclude others.

It is also important to recognize the difference in leadership styles between the various Hispanic cultures. For example, the Puerto Rican style tends to be very aggressive, with debate and discussion, while the Mexican style is more indirect and informal. These differences in the psychology of leadership must be taken into account during training.

Second-generation leaders need to understand how power works and how the church can work with the power structures of a city. They need to understand the issues facing first-generation immigrants such as citizenship, bilingual education, welfare, and how to vote. They must have the ability to empower.

Another issue raised by Canales is that of emerging Hispanic leaders who are undocumented immigrants. They may be gifted, but they can rise only so far in leadership at the institutional or denominational level because of their undocumented status. The difficult question to wrestle with is this: How can a church work with potential leaders who feel a strong call to ministry but have to deal with the frustration and fear of being undocumented? Or, for those who are documented, how can the church help them overcome the feeling of being second class because they may not yet be full-fledged citizens?

**Dr. Alvaro Nieves**
**Chicago Puerto Rican (Salvation Army)**

The first consideration in developing second-generation leaders, Nieves feels, is to determine the levels at which leadership development can occur. Analyzing the situation in which the leader will work will help pastors identify requirements for leadership in that context. Then they could implement a training program followed by an evaluation of the leaders and programs. The evaluation phase is especially important in the initial stages of development, and it may be formative or summative in nature. It may involve in-house staff, outside evaluators or both.

A second consideration is to assess the potential leader's motivational force. How motivated are they to apply themselves to the development process? Extreme caution should be used, however, so as not to blame the victim for apparent failures or inadequacies. There may be other reasons.

The local congregation should also undergo a specific needs analysis so that it can design a strategy adapted to the local scene, and training can be in tune with that design.

Beyond the local church, new leaders should seek more general training at the regional, conference, presbytery, denominational and ecumenical levels. Although it may be possible to utilize case study material, emphasis at this stage should be placed on generalized skills, techniques and methods. It is imperative that leaders gain an awareness of structural issues. A lack of structural awareness can lead to acts of prejudice (especially at the denominational level) such as blaming the victim for lack of motivation, intelligence, ability, etc., when limited opportunity and access structures are responsible. Denominational leaders must also be educated. They cannot use the same techniques to train minority leaders— not because Puerto Ricans or blacks are incapable but because the denomination does not understand their context.

As pastors work to develop leaders, they must address the issue of identity conflict. Instilling a sense of pride in whatever ethnicity the leaders are is vital. We have to give both ourselves and each other permission to be Puerto Rican or Cuban or Mexican. The church has done damage by promoting an assimilation model, that is, urging leaders to become more American or more white. And when we choose to embrace our ethnic heritage, we are accused of being militant or arrogant.

Our perception of reality is tied inextricably to language. As second-generation leaders, we must stop apologizing that our written Spanish is not as good as we would like. We can still be bilingual and bicultural. The third generation, who knows less Spanish than we do, will be ridiculed even more.

We as a people are not very familiar with our own literature and history. As a result, we fail to acknowledge the historical realities we have in common with other Hispanic cultures. For example, the United States was illegally trespassing on Mexican property. They fought for it, won the war, and made a treaty which guaranteed, among other things, the right for Mexicans living in the territory won by the United States to retain the Spanish language and land ownership. Both of these guaranteed rights were almost immediately broken. Sadly, Puerto Rican children in New York identify more with Davy Crockett than with the Mexicans at the Alamo.

### The Reverend Josue Abreu
### South Florida Cuban (Christian Reformed Church)

The second-generation Cuban population in south Florida is unique, Abreu claims. These young people are extremely influenced by their parents' culture, yet because they have been educated in this country, they are influenced by North American culture as well. In education they are North American, but in cultural expression at home they are Cuban. Both dynamics are working and must be considered when evangelizing the second generation.

It is also clear, however, that many do not know exactly how to identify with their culture. For example, in political discussions, Cuban-Americans speak about Cuba as though they were the ones who lost their homes and businesses there. But the reality is that they have been raised in the U.S., and the Cuban discussion really belongs to their parents or recent immigrants. Somewhere between these two developmental influences, they need to identify their own personality and perspective on life.

Much of this is true for all Hispanic national groups. However, I believe the uniqueness of the Cuban-Americans Abreu refers to arises from the thriving Cuban ethnic enclave in south Florida which continually reinforces its ties to first-generation refugees and immigrants.

The enclave dynamic also provides understanding for the issue of language. Even though second-generation Cubans are educated and fluent in English, after high school most of them see the need to maintain fluency in Spanish as well and are truly bilingual. In Abreu's words, "They understand that Spanish is a good thing to follow, and try to keep it. They see value in being bilingual." Therefore, they can be reached for the Lord in either language.

Religion is another area in which we must be sensitive. Most of those who arrived from Cuba were Catholic but rarely attended church. In chapter two we saw that many priests joined the initial wave of refugees fleeing Castro's regime, and they made themselves available to the people. But with the continuing waves of Cuban immigrants, the population grew faster than the places to worship. With a lack of churches and parents who probably didn't attend church anyway, second-generation young adults know almost nothing about the church, Catholic or evangelical. In Abreu's words, they are "completely blank." Evangelism, therefore, will have to begin by building relationships and good friendships.

Another pastor in the south Florida area recognized this same problem. He pointed out that while missionaries have been sent to South and Central America and the Caribbean to reach the poor people, the church has not been able to reach those Cubans who came here twenty-five years ago. He also offered some words of caution to Anglo denominations that want to minister in Hispanic communities. The philosophy of ministry must be committed to the Hispanic—not the North American—culture. Also, denominational requirements for training should be reevaluated in order to train second-generation Hispanic leaders. They need quality training but within a different system. Too many denominations ask people to commit to one system, and that is wrong. Systems are not permanent, and they must be changed when necessary.

This pastor also warned Anglo denominations to face the damage they are doing by not adequately training their urban Anglo ministers, many of whom are leaving the city behind. First, the departure produces a sense of abandonment among the Hispanics, who then turn to other arenas, such as politics. Second, it fosters materialism, because the deserted church facilities are often sold to nonchurch groups rather than turned over to a Hispanic congregation which would maintain a Christian witness in the changing community. This materialism must be confronted in order for denominations to see and meet the needs of Hispanics, without a paternalistic overtone.

### The Reverend H. O. Espinoza
### San Antonio Mexican-American (Church of the Nazarene)

All Hispanic leaders would agree on Espinoza's first observation: that Hispanic young people need to find their identity as North Americans while also taking into account their different background cultures and subcultures. They must struggle to come to terms with their parents' culture, even if the parents are second generation. According to anthropological studies, the second and third generations struggle more than others in determining their place. Espinoza thinks that the greatest challenge for Hispanic leadership is to help the second and third generation "find their place in the mosaic in this society, a very plastic and liquid society."

Related to the identity issue is the need for good role models, specifically, leaders oriented to the needs and circumstances of Hispanics in the U.S. Most Hispanic leaders, especially Protestants, are oriented toward Latin America. Only a few outstanding Hispanic leaders remain—most of whom are U.S.-born—to serve as role models for our young people. Ninety to ninety-five percent of the Latin American born leaders are Latin American oriented.

Espinoza echoes the concerns of the other leaders in regard to bilingualism. He asks, "Where do we fit with using two languages? How much can we let go of the Spanish language without losing our Hispanic culture and heritage?" An organization called the Hispanic Association for Bilingual Bicultural Ministries (HABBM) has been established to deal with just this kind of question.

Another issue in the Southwest is the growing number of Hispanics in the large Anglo churches. In San Antonio, the fastest-growing Protestant Anglo church is over one-third Hispanic, and those Hispanics are second-, third- and fourth-generation young people. Generally speaking, the churches winning the second and third generation for Christ are not Hispanic but Anglo. This again raises the issue of identity.

Education continues to be a problem. We must challenge and encourage our young people not only to seek better education, but also to pursue financial aid options. We need to open doors for our young people. Role models can help a great deal here.

The Roman Catholic background of most Hispanics remains an issue. "We don't generally realize how Roman Catholic we still are even though we are Protestant," Espinoza states. His family has been Protestant since 1860, but he still carries much Catholic baggage within himself, especially in the deterministic way he looks at things. "It comes out in phrases such as, 'If I am poor, it's the will of God.' It is a very fatalistic view. 'I am this or that because it is my *destino* (destiny).' Not because of culture, parents, or personal habits, but because it's God's will." Espinoza indicates that this is pure Catholic, "pure St. Augustine." Another piece of Catholic baggage—one that has continued for many generations—is a high degree of suspicion toward others. Many Hispanics have difficulty trusting people. The Protestant culture is just the opposite: They tend to trust people, to believe people, and to believe in their own efforts. These are subtle problems in the Hispanic culture that the second and third generations need to recognize in themselves and in their children. Espinoza feels that Hispanic Protestants have not really struggled with the effects of their Catholic roots.

On the one hand, second-generation Hispanics need to remember the past; but on the other hand, they cannot be oriented toward the past. They must become future oriented, particularly at this time in history when the whole world is changing—governments, philosophies, even the geographic world. It is a very challenging time to open the eyes of young people. No other Hispanic generation has had the opportunities and challenges that the second and third generations do now. Using Revelation 21:5 as a framework, Espinoza explains how God is currently making a new people here in the U.S. In one hundred years a brand new culture will emerge, just as a new *mestizo* culture arose centuries ago when the Spaniards came to America and mixed with the Indians. Even now, God is allowing the subcultures to mix with each other as well as with Anglos and blacks, and he is making a new race. It is upon these new generations of Hispanic young people that the burden, the challenge and the opportunity have fallen. That is where we need the leadership. States Espinoza: "God is taking us out of another Egypt and into another promised land, and so we need Moseses and Joshuas."

**Summary**

As we consider the part we can play in developing second-generation Hispanic leaders, we can draw upon the insights given in this chapter by experienced, reputable leaders who are rooted in their culture. Since each of them emphasized the language issue, we should further investigate the bilingual dimensions of training, even though many will not have what some Hispanics consider an adequate handle on the Spanish language. Nieves suggests we not blame the victim for his or her problems, as that will hinder our attempts to work with second- and third-generation leaders. Cortés noted that the process of training and selecting leaders is often informal, but he hopes for a more efficient, intentional way of training in the future. Alicea worries that we might be losing some of our most talented leaders to other ethnic ministries that will not use them as well. Finally, we must remember that nearly all leaders emerge from the local church and are trained by what Cortés calls "learning as you go and do."

# Chapter 9

---

# Leadership
# Development

I t is now time to examine in more detail the process of developing leaders among second- and third-generation Hispanics. First-generation Hispanic leaders traditionally have taken a different route to ordination and ministerial preparation than leaders in Anglo churches. The usual course of events for Anglo pastors is formal education, Bible college, seminary, then ordination and ministry. Hispanics both here in the U.S. and in Latin America have approached this process differently. The route usually begins by potential leaders proving themselves in the local church while becoming "faithful members." The pastor pays closer attention to these individuals, considers them to be dependable, and entrusts them with additional responsibilities. They may teach, work with youth, lead services, coordinate ministries, and preach periodically. The training takes place while doing ministry, and the need for education is triggered by actual hands-on involvement.

Eventually the mother church formally affirms their calling, ordains them, and establishes an independent ministry for them to lead. Very often these young leaders have been building a nucleus of believers that will become a new church.

This pattern of proving one's calling in the context of the local church is usually the recommended process for approaching the ministry in the Hispanic community. In his research on theological education for Hispanics, Justo González notes,

> Hispanic ministers do not follow the route of choosing the ministry, going to seminary, being ordained, and then becoming ministers, which is typical in the white church. Most of them are already in ministry when they decide they need further education.[1]

It is not a deliberate process, but rather a dynamic that naturally occurs in the church as the Spirit leads. On the other hand, it would not be unwise for potential Hispanic ministers to attend seminary or Bible college first, but only after they have shown serious commitment to God's work and feel called to serve him full time. How often we dismiss the challenge for Hispanics to attend academic institutions for further education and development. I agree with González that Hispanics need "more, not less, academic and intellectual tools."[2]

In the introduction of *Frontiers of Hispanic Theology in the U.S.* Allan Figueroa Deck writes,

> Until now there have been few professional United States Hispanic theological voices. Virgil Elizondo, within the Roman Catholic tradition, and Justo González and Orlando Costas, within the Protestant tradition, are among the few who come to mind.[3]

This is alarming but true. (I imagine that Deck is limiting his list of theologians to those who have written and published theological works.) There is a great need for theological and ecclesiastical leaders who will give proper guidance to the Hispanic community. But where will we find them, if not from among the faithful second-

and third-generation young people in our churches?

So far, the most effective model is one in which the Hispanic local church takes on the challenge of developing second-generation leadership. The model does not discourage formal theological education, but primarily depends on the resources God has given the local church.

There are four main principles to follow in engaging and developing second-generation Hispanic leadership: building a theological framework that is appropriate for the second generation, building relationships, building servants, and building a selection process.

## Building a Theological Framework

Contextualization, in simple terms, is the effort to make the biblical text relevant to our present social reality.[4] We are to communicate God's written Word to a unique context without relativizing the truth of God's Word. It is the "engagement between at least two sets of horizons, namely that of the ancient text and that of modern hearer or reader."[5]

> Above all, we need to know and use contextualization in order to present the gospel in such a way that our contemporaries will see the relevance of this message for their personal and social needs.[6]

Contextualization is an ongoing process, one that applies not only to a changing world, but also to a changing church. Too often contextualizers have directed so much attention to communicating the gospel to the outside world that they have, at times, ignored the needs and changing realities of the church.

One such situation is the generational transition in the Hispanic church. In this case, contextualization efforts are more inward and generational than outward and evangelistic. The growing stability of Hispanics in North America will no doubt provide a stratum of people who are engaging a new reality, one different than that of their parents and more in tune with the present political social framework of the urban context. These generational distinctives are as much a task of contextualization as that of a completely different culture. I often think the process is *more* difficult and challenging because we are tempted to believe our culture is not changing since our surname, color and basic cultural traits are still the same. We somehow overlook the dynamic changes occurring within our own culture. Without this awareness, our philosophy of ministry may lead us to ignore the second and third generation.

How can we effectively incorporate this new growing generation into the Hispanic church? Is there room for change or contextualization of ministry in the existing Hispanic church to prepare and use the second- and third-generation Hispanic population? There are at least seven areas to consider:

1. Worldviews—ways of viewing the world
2. Cognitive processes—ways of thinking
3. Linguistic forms—ways of expressing ideas
4. Behavioral patterns—ways of acting
5. Communication media—ways of channeling the message
6. Social structures—ways of interacting
7. Motivational sources—ways of deciding[7]

Even though we are basically rooted in the same culture, the context and historical situation call for another look at our congregation. How are the second and third generation viewing the world? Is it more urban than rural? More global and multiethnic than homogeneous? Their thinking process is unique, influenced by the present age and setting. Certainly their expression of life and faith will take on new symbols of communication. Their lifestyle patterns will challenge the existing monolingual, monocultural church and often be criticized as "worldly" rather than accepted as a new expression of thinking and communicating. These matters must be taken under consideration.

I see several encouraging dimensions that appear to touch every level of the Hispanic church. One is a hunger and respect for the authority of the Word, an appetite to understand and communicate the Scriptures. We look to the Word often for answers to common and mysterious questions of life. And we realize that we must not only know the Bible, but we must live the Word in a right relationship to God. For Hispanics—both Roman Catholic and Protestant—the Bible is the Word of God; therefore, they are more easily motivated to teach and learn from the Scriptures.

Another encouraging aspect is our willingness to obey. Hispanics view the Bible as applying to real life situations. They do not intellectualize the Word or find proof texts to support a theoretical position; they primarily use it to guide them in their everyday life as Christians. This gives teachers an edge in communicating God's truth.

What happens when contextualization is ignored by the church? Gilliland warns, "The Bible is not brought to bear upon local problems, the meaning of conversion for all of life is not explored, the means for spiritual growth are not utilized nor are responsibilities taken seriously."[8] Contextualization, as he puts it, "guards against the imperialism of theology."[9] I have rarely found apathy for the Scriptures in the Christian Hispanic community. So we should continue to teach and encourage others to study the Word of God. Seminary and formal training should also be encouraged. González notes that "there is a need for better education combined with the desire for recognition."[10]

Surely we will need to overcome many obstacles in our theological institutions such as racism, overdependence on Eurocentric theology, and, last but not least, required knowledge of Greek and Hebrew. Here I would not be as firm as González, but I would agree with the observation of a Pentecostal pastor studying Greek: "If I am going to devote my entire life to expounding this text, I better be able to read it."[11] In spite of these obstacles, I would still encourage the initiation of a theological training program for emerging leaders—preferably institutional learning that promotes not only biblical theology but also contextualization.

**Building Relationships**

There are five important aspects to building relationships:

*147*

*1. Mutuality.* A relationship must be mutually desired. It is not imposed, but rather enjoyed and desired over time. Sometimes the friendship occurs immediately, but more often it requires numerous personal contacts before one wishes to be more involved. It is a reciprocal model that enriches both parties; both are sharing their lives together. The Scriptures provide such an inclusive dimension. We are all attaining to unity of faith (Eph 4:13), we are all disciples, Christ is the one who teaches us (Mt 23:10), we are all being transformed into his image (2 Cor 3:18), we are all called to go and make disciples (Mt 28:19-20), we are all to be witnesses for Christ (Acts 1:8), we are in need of each other (1 Cor 12:21-26). We are to exercise our spiritual gifts (Eph 4:10-11) out of mutual concern, and submit to one another as we yield to God's lordship (Eph 5:21). In other words, Christian living and growth take place in reciprocity, as we build relationships. Hispanics care less about institutional commitments and more about commitments to relationships and community.

*2. Holism.* The second aspect is a whole-life relationship, meaning that we should not separate the social from the spiritual but rather see God as involved in the totality of life. I have found that times of casual, relaxed discussions and recreational activities can be the most important part of building a relationship. We are not as protective of self, and we feel free to disclose more of who we are. We share many sides of our personalities that we do not often reveal in "spiritual" moments. This allows for an interweaving of two lives. Working together or visiting the sick can be great times for sharing and learning.

Whole-life relationships must go both ways. Just as we enter into the everyday life of others, we should also allow others to see our daily life and family interaction. As ministers, our credibility to a second-generation Hispanic will dramatically increase when he or she can examine our family life and our daily walk, not just our preaching and teaching. Praying and sharing Scripture is good, but it is not enough. We must bring people into our life, not just that

148

segment that we erroneously call ministry. Jesus "became flesh and made his dwelling among us" (Jn 1:14). That is, he lived out his life as a servant, in appearance as a man, humbling himself (Phil 2:8). His ministry was not separated from his life. His life in action *was* his ministry.

In Scripture we find that the Gospel is essentially the person and work of Jesus Christ. It is not a message or formulation, but the person Jesus Christ. There are several features of his incarnation which are imporant considerations for the communication of the Gospel:

*Incarnation is specific to a context.* Jesus did not come as a universal man: he came as a Jew to Jews. Incarnation is limited to a context, it is not general and universal.

*Incarnation is involved in a context.* Jesus did not just speak to Jews, he became a Jew. He identified himself with all aspects of being a Jew.

*Incarnation takes the cultural context seriously.* Jesus did not become a Jew as a convenient illustration of general truths. He faced real problems, debates, issues, struggles and conflicts which concerned the Jewish people. He entered into sharp debate with the Pharisees and Sadducees about how to be obedient to God. He took the side of social outcasts, the women, the Samaritans, and the lepers. Within that real Jewish culture, its economic, social and political relationships, he was incarnate.

*Incarnation takes humanity seriously.* Jesus did not address the Jews impersonally, as one abstracted from their cultural context. He came to his own, and spelt out his claims in terms that spoke uniquely to Jews—their social, economic and political relationships, not just their personal rights and religious beliefs. The Jew's holistic view of life as ordered under God admitted no such division. Jesus addressed himself to economic questions, to the political groupings in Israel, and relationships of injustice that prevailed.

On these issues his concern was not so much *effectiveness,* in terms of winning a large following, as *authenticity,* that people should clearly understand the nature of his mission and of God's Kingdom.[12]

When Jesus calms the storm in Luke 8:22-25, we learn a lot about him. Not only is he Jesus, the tired person who needed a nap, but he is also the sovereign Lord who "rebuked the wind and the raging waters" (8:24). 'Where is your faith?' he asked his disciples. In fear and amazement they asked one another, " 'Who is this? He commands even the winds and the water, and they obey him' " (8:25). Jesus used daily circumstances to teach. Sometimes these circumstances were intense, as in the storm, and other times they were quite ordinary. We can take a similar approach in our own contemporary situation. Intense and faithful relationships can and should be built wholistically if we are living among the people we are serving. Incarnation is important to developing relationships.

*3. Listening Ability.* Another significant aspect of relationship-building is learning to listen. Myron Rush says,

> When I first got into the consulting business, I assumed that the key to good communication was one's ability to verbalize his thoughts and feelings. Over the years, I've changed my thinking. I now believe that the key is the ability to be a good listener.[13]

Interestingly, the very opposite tends to occur when missionaries or pastors work with emerging leaders. Pastors do the talking, and the trainee is expected to listen. Paulo Freire speaks of this dimension in educational terms which ultimately dehumanize the students. Several indicators are

(a) the teacher teaches and the students are taught;

(b) the teacher knows everything and the students know nothing;

(c) the teacher thinks and the students are thought about;

(d) the teacher talks and the students listen—meekly.[14]

This attitude may damage potentially fruitful relationships. No one has everything to give and nothing to receive. Again we are reminded of the need for reciprocity. It may be more important for the missionary or pastor to listen first so that he can learn to receive and feel mutual worth. Listening provides an environment in which others can be who they are and express their uniqueness without fear of rejection. "Listening is the key to developing understanding."[15] It requires concentration and undivided attention. To do otherwise is to manipulate the situation, causing the other to wonder if they are really important to you. Listening involves respecting the other person as an individual made in God's image and significant to God's mission. Rush indicates that there are two kinds of listening—perceptive and passive. Perceptive listening focuses on what is behind the verbal and nonverbal message. It listens "for the thoughts and feelings."[16] Passive listening merely takes in the words themselves, and often leads to misunderstanding. Perceptive listeners must "have an honest desire to hear what the speaker is saying." They should provide feedback "to assure the sender you have heard correctly, and the sender will be responsible to say so if you have not." An important part of the feedback is to make sure you are not judging the message.[17]

As Christian leaders, we are trained to speak and not to listen. We've been programmed to believe that listening is not leading, not taking responsibility, not being productive. So we keep on talking. We urgently need to learn how to listen. Rush gives us several rules for effective listening:

a. Don't interrupt the speaker.

b. Don't start forming your response while the speaker is still talking.

c. Do ask questions for clarity.

d. Don't assume you already know what the speaker is going to say.[18]

*4. Honesty.* In building relationships, not only is it important to be reciprocal, holistic and a listener, it is also important to be honest. Failing or making a mistake in public may have more positive fruit than expected. Emerging leaders, who often feel inferior to their mentors, may recognize that we all have much to learn. Normally we hope that developing leaders will not discover our frailties and shortcomings. But hiding them tends to make our position look impossible to reach. The apostle Paul, in contrast, expresses himself openly: "I came to you in weakness and fear, and with much trembling" (1 Cor 2:3). Rather than cover up who we are, honestly sharing ourselves will more likely enhance our relationships. It also helps us to learn how to be honest without being arrogant or damaging to the spirit of those we are serving. Paul tells us, "Therefore each of you must put off falsehood and speak truthfully to his neighbor, for we are all members of one body" (Eph 4:25). Though it is easy to admit that honesty belongs in every relationship, it is not very easy to accomplish.

5. *Patience.* When it comes to building relationships, we cannot rush matters. Emerging leaders may not yet be ready. Patience allows for a healthy, growing environment. In fact, all of the previous four aspects of relationship building require patience, because they all take time. The ability to listen is cultivated and learned in process. Honesty takes trust, and trust grows with time. In some ways relationship-building is never-ending. We simply move from one phase to another.

While there are many other aspects to building relationships, I have tried to zero in on the ones most important to the process of leadership development. And we must always keep in mind that we are disciples together and that Christ is our teacher (Mt 23:10).

Among second-generation Hispanics, our methods may have to be adjusted to each person. In some cases inner contact may take longer than expected. Certain cultures respond to relationships differently, and it is wise to review the cultural dimensions on how to enter this process. People will not want to be viewed as a "target audience," but rather as human beings with many needs who desire respect and compassion. They do not care about theological paradigms or concepts as much as they want to know that we care for them. Compassion requires solidarity, a "suffering with." Vulnerability must be mutual. It is imperative that we live in the community and participate in its life, using the same stores, schools and means of recreation. We are as enriched and as limited as they are. We begin to internalize their suffering and powerlessness.

## Building Servants

In developing second-generation Hispanic leaders within the church, our direct participation is essential. The following steps highlight the various roles we will need to play in building mature and fruitful new leaders. All of them involve dialogue as part of the process.

*Modeling:* Allowing emerging leaders to observe *our* life and ministry, how we live out the gospel in context, followed by dialogue.

*Supervision:* Directing and overseeing young leaders as they live out the gospel and carry on ministry, followed by dialogue.

*Cognitive input:* Teaching, lecturing, providing formal and informal means of instruction, with sufficient dialogue.

*Observing others:* Going outside of community, state and country to see the global dimensions of God's work in the world.

*Sending:* Assigning new leaders to various missions endeavors, allowing them to do ministry in their unique way while keeping biblical principles intact.

Each of these steps will be considered in the context of second-generation Hispanics. In some cases, steps occur simultaneously rather than in chronological order.

*1. Modeling.* Observing is something we all do, yet it is also a skill that needs to be taught. Spradley tells us that "we are all *observers*, even when acting as ordinary participants. But what we watch and listen for remains limited to our immediate purpose of accomplishing some activity."[19] Because we do not observe as closely as we should, it is easy to miss much of what is happening. One way to teach observation is by setting up situations where we model good leadership, and then questioning or dialoguing with the prospective leaders afterwards. For example, after we witness to a person on the street, we can ask questions such as, What did you notice about the person I was speaking to? What was their culture? What socioeconomic range were they in? Were they single, married, a parent? Were they receptive to the gospel? Why or why not? What were the felt needs of that individual? Why did I use a particular passage of Scripture and specific words to communicate? How would you do it and why?

The young leaders must learn to observe with all their senses. It is not enough to see; they must develop perceptive listening skills so they can pick up on various needs and truths about the individual. Sometimes these needs are immediate and should not be ignored. For example, a woman we are speaking with mentions she is going to the clinic with her child. The clinic is two miles away and she is expected at a certain time, but she has no means of transportation. A ride to the clinic may be the most constructive initial approach to sharing the gospel. Or, if parents strike up a conversation about the needs of their children's education, we should take time to listen and respond to their concerns. If we are not observant, we will insensitively push ahead with our agenda without considering the immediate need of the individual.

One resource that gives some help in understanding human needs (though it should not dictate our understanding of biblical teaching on human nature) is Maslow's Hierarchy of Human Motives, which, to be best used, will also need cultural accountability. Notice that the needs get more basic as we go down the list:

7. Aesthetic needs
6. Desire to know and understand
5. Need for self-actualization
4. Esteem needs
    a. self-esteem
    b. esteem from others
3. Love and belongingness needs
2. Safety needs
1. Physiological needs

Maslow's basic point in his theory and model is that *all* seven of these needs are intrinsic to human personality—but not all of them are center stage, in the forefront of consciousness, and *currently* motivating a person's life. The need that is in the forefront of consciousness and that is currently motivating the individual will be the lowest need that is basically unfulfilled.

For instance, the basic, rock-bottom human needs are physiological—nutrition, elimination, sex, sleep. If these needs are not met, a person spends most of his time in an attempt to fulfill them; and until these physiological needs are met, he ignores his other needs that are present in the background of his personality. In wartime, when people are starving and homeless, they do not expend much energy asking philosophical questions or painting landscapes.[20]

After modeling some aspect of ministry, we can initiate dialogue with questions that teach the emerging leader observing skills. We can first ask how the emerging leader might have handled the situation. Why witness? Does God have a concern for the whole person? Much of the dialogue falls under the heading of theological and missiological understanding for the purpose of praxis. The discussion will often lead into contextualization and help an emerging leader become a capable contextualist.

In cases where it may be impossible to have the young leader with us, we can still share what we are doing. For example, much of the training we give in counseling would be covered in cognitive teaching form using case studies. But we can also train our young people in observation by sharing about our own preparation and expressing the feelings we experience during counseling. Counseling is not merely an academic discipline, but rather a shepherding aspect of ministry that involves the pastor deeply, requires compassion, and often brings about stress.

We can also share on a personal level about private aspects of ministry, such as preparing messages. We can talk about how we selected the theme, developed the ideas and exegeted the Scriptures, and what response we desired. We can also share the strain and inadequacy we may have felt during the preparation, the constraints of time, perhaps even the spiritual battle that led us to profound prayer.

Our observation training should not be limited to areas of ministry that run smoothly, but should also include areas that involve conflict and stress. Emerging leaders must also observe how we handle matters of discipline, forgiveness and reconciliation. Because modeling is so important in helping others learn observation skills, the privatistic lifestyle fostered in North American culture often hinders leadership development.

*2. Supervision.* The basic idea here is to reverse the roles in step one. This time the emerging leader does ministry, and the missionary or pastor does the observing in order to provide supervision and guidance. Young leaders need to practice what they have been learning from observing the pastor at work. A key aspect of supervision is knowing how much responsibility to give the new leader and when. It can be destructive to allow the individual to do too much too soon. Most second-generation leaders should begin by learning to share their faith, lead a person to Christ and conduct the early stages of discipleship. The missionary or pastor must observe his young people closely to identify personality traits that need healing or restructuring under the lordship of Christ. For example, the way leaders handle finances and manage their homes will directly affect their ability to serve. Many pastors have fallen short in their ministry because of domestic mismanagement. Supervision will enable us to pinpoint areas that need special resources and attention. In this way we will assist the growth of the emerging leaders and broaden their ministerial responsibilities.

Here are a few guidelines for supervision:

a. Begin with acts of ministry that will not produce ego trips and puff up the individual to the point of grieving the Holy Spirit. Emerging leaders should be deeply aware of the sovereign God's involvement in salvation and service, and humility should result. Also, as responsibilities increase, we should monitor their levels of anxiety and fear of failure, which can cause them to avoid or postpone getting involved.

b. Observe attitudes as they relate to submission and authority, and attitudes toward service that call for seemingly unimportant or behind-the-scenes tasks. Do they view setting up the chairs or cleaning the restrooms as someone else's job, or do they willingly pitch in as the Lord's servants? Attitudes toward family should be noted and evaluated. Many emerging leaders will come from hurting families with a history of poor relationships. They must be encouraged to love and honor their families, even when they disagree with their approach to life.

c. Watch their teamwork. Are they lone-ranger types, or do they work well with others? Leaders must be able to work well on a team. The ability is best learned by watching others and then by practicing it themselves at various levels of ministry. Those with no role models or previous team experience will have greater difficulty accepting and delegating responsibilities and maintaining an overall spirit of cooperation.

d. Observe their stewardship as they accomplish their tasks. Note the quality of the work and how long it took. Are they responsible and accountable for their use of time and resources? How well do they evaluate their own accomplishments? Young leaders who are truly concerned about their calling will strive to take responsibility for their assignments. And as they mature, they can take on more responsibility.

3. *Cognitive Input.* Intellectual training can occur at two levels, informal-local and formal. Local is primarily an in-community teaching situation; formal is an institutional approach involving seminaries or Bible schools. The informal-local approach can take place in a home or church in a weekly two- or three-hour block of time. For example, a two-hour Sunday-school class can be used for leadership training. Informal does not mean structureless. The two-hour class should be well structured, and the participants should be serious about the training and sharing. The teaching

could revolve around case studies written by the leaders or by the pastor or missionary. These case studies should reflect common situations in the local community. From there, discuss the biblical and pastoral implications. Or the pastor could assign each young leader to present a ministry issue they are facing or a theological theme they are wrestling with, and the group could discuss it together.

The formal approach to training is more difficult for Hispanic leaders. A nearby seminary may be able to provide courses in community that will help students do theology in an urban context. Unfortunately, many religious institutions lack the ability to contextualize the content and be sensitive to the culture. And some seminaries have a banking concept of education which just provides information in lectures. Instruction is "deposited" in students as money is deposited in a bank. It is one-way, and the content is often detached from the real world of the student.[21]

Narration (with the teacher as narrator) leads the students to memorize mechanically the narrated content. Worse yet, it turns them into "containers," into "receptacles" to be "filled" by the teacher. The more completely they fill the receptacles, the better teachers they are. The more meekly the receptacles permit themselves to be filled, the better students they are.[22]

This problem can be overcome if the community is valued in the educational process. Excellent models of this are the Center for Urban Ministerial Education (CUME) in Boston and the Center for Urban Theological Studies (CUTS) in Philadelphia.

Justo González has addressed the concern of some that academic tools and training are inappropriate for Hispanics because we are either academically inferior due to our history or we are more concerned with practice:

Hispanics need more, not less, academic and intellectual tools. While theological education must continue at all levels, we must take care not to fall into the trap of thinking that because most of the Hispanic constituency has had few educational opportunities a mediocre education suffices for ministry among them.[23]

4. *Observing Others.* Many of our community leaders have an "island" mentality—that is, they confine their focus and experience to a given geographic area. Many will never leave their immediate community boundaries during their lifetime. In ministry this mentality limits the exposure of young leaders to new experiences and resources for growth. It also omits the global picture of missions. Leaders need multiethnic, multicultural, domestic and foreign experiences in order to evaluate different approaches to ministry from outside the community. They should take field trips both within the city and out of state to observe how others are doing ministry. They should interact with those they visit, with one another and with their pastors, comparing and critiquing how ministry is accomplished in different contexts. And occasional trips outside the U.S. will give them a fuller understanding of global mission. Every experience, every discussion, becomes a learning event.

5. *Sending.* This aspect of developing emerging leaders allows them to begin a ministry apart from the mentor without being completely independent of him or her. New leaders learn to seek and share with the mentor for their own growth and development. They are neither dependent nor fully independent, but rather interdependent. At this juncture emerging leaders must face the responsibility of finding and using their own ministry resources. Roland Allen describes how this process must have occurred in the Bible:

> With the appointment of elders the churches were complete. They were fully equipped. They very soon became familiar with all the orders of ministry both permanent and charismatic. They no longer depended necessarily upon St Paul. If he went away, or if he died, the churches remained. They grew in numbers and in grace: they were centres of spiritual light by which the darkness of surrounding heathenism was gradually dispelled. In Galatia "the churches were strengthened in the faith and increased in number daily." From Thessalonica "the word of the

Lord sounded out" in Macedonia and Achaia. From Ephesus the Gospel spread throughout all the neighbouring country so that many churches sprang up, the members of which had never seen St Paul's face, and he himself could write to the Romans that he had "no more place in those regions."

They were no longer dependent upon the Apostle, but they were not independent of him.[24]

Meetings with the emerging leaders should be scheduled and organized. A commitment to meeting is important and should be expected. This will help them work into ministry gradually. There is a wide gap between dependent and independent ministry. Things that were done before under supervision and were accomplished with confidence and joy now have become extremely difficult. The emerging leaders' confidence may be shaken and their joy inconsistent. During this time the mentor reviews preaching and teaching messages and interacts on all levels of ministry. Most important, the mentor provides support. As the new leader's confidence builds, the mentor's role shifts to become primarily a resource who is called upon when needed. Meetings are less frequent and voluntary. And on occasion, the mentor may even call the new leader for resources.

### Building a Selection Process

In selecting and working with second-generation Hispanics in various Chicago ministries, I noticed eight important characteristics to look for in potential leaders. (These characteristics are general enough to be considered for most ministries.)

*1. Willingness.* A potential leader must have an appetite to learn, a willingness to follow, an openness to new possibilities, and a desire to grow. Too often we look for leaders who are already trained and prepared by others. I have found that indigenous people who are trained for ministry by their missionaries or pastors are more effective and make a permanent commitment to their community. Pastors need to watch for and cultivate young hearts to be enthusiastic and willing to follow the Lord in the future. We need young people with the same willingness as Levi: " 'Follow me,' Jesus said to him, and Levi got up, left everything and followed him" (Lk 5:27-28).

2. *Moldability*. How teachable are the potential leaders? Can they trust God and others with their lives? If so, they are probably open to change and to new or old ideas. They are likely able to submit to authority and be convicted of sin. I believe Paul was a moldable person. "Together Barnabas and Paul taught. Here again Barnabas played a mentoring role wherein he took the lead but also provided opportunities for Paul to learn and grow over the period of a year."[25]

3. *Servant attitude*. Willingness and moldability need to be integrated with the biblical attitude of servanthood. Jesus said that servanthood was the most important requirement to follow him: "If anyone wants to be first, he must be the very last, and the servant of all" (Mk 9:35). "For even the Son of Man did not come to be served, but to serve, and to give his life as a ransom for many" (Mk 10:45).

Much of the New Testament notion of service deals with provision of food and drink for the hungry and thirsty, shelter for the homeless, clothes for the naked and destitute, visitation of the sick and imprisoned, care for widows and orphans. In Matthew 25:45, Jesus said that not serving "the least of these" in these ways is a failure to do it to him. Many are trained to oppose such service rather than to embrace it in fulfillment of the Lord's will. Often much teaching on servanthood has to be done in order to keep it within the biblical framework. I have noticed that recent converts are more willing to serve others than the more "mature" Christians, who seem to feel that as Christians grow they depart from servanthood. How does one teach the willingness to serve? Primarily by modeling servanthood and by discussing the potential leader's commitment to service.

4. *Urban crosscultural attitudes and abilities*. Because the urban

context is where the second-generation Hispanic leader will minister, he or she must possess sufficient urban crosscultural attitudes and abilities. It is interesting to remember that the second-generation Hispanic has acquired a bicultural, bilingual trait.

Although such a high percentage of Hispanics are born in the United States, a very large percentage also report that Spanish is the language spoken at home. Eleven million people, or 75% of all Hispanics counted by the census, reported that Spanish is the language spoken at home. (Again, this does not include the 3.2 million population of Puerto Rico.) Roughly one fourth of those who speak Spanish at home, or 19% of the Hispanic population, also declared that they do not speak English well, or that they do not speak it at all. There is no statistic regarding the use of Spanish by the 25% of Hispanics who declared that English is the language most used at home. It is likely that roughly half of these are bilingual, or have at least some use of Spanish. Thus, it would appear that the usage of language among Hispanics in the United States breaks down as follows:

English only 12.5%
Bilingual with English preference 12.5%
Bilingual with Spanish preference 56.0%
Spanish only 19.0%

Since any undercounting by the census is most likely to have taken place among undocumented Hispanics, and these would tend to speak Spanish either exclusively or primarily, it would seem that the number of Hispanics who do not use Spanish at all is 10% or less of the total Hispanic population. Thus, bilingualism is likely to continue being a feature of the Hispanic community in the foreseeable future.[26]

Also, many Puerto Ricans in Chicago and New York City have grown up in African-American communities and have acquired many linguistic and cultural traits of that community. The potential leader must be keen on urban crosscultural issues and should move toward developing those skills.

*5. Team orientation.* Another important characteristic is the need to consider team-oriented ministry. A person should seek others with whom to work. In the city it is crucial to value the organism of the church and move toward a nonclergy-dominated team.

> Almost all church theology is clerical; almost always ordained ministers in seminaries or in congregations are called upon to depict the meaning of the Christian life in any profound way. [Therefore, the laity is usually omitted from] the circles out of which theological interpretation of life occurs.[27]

In a team approach, working coequally with others provides a healthy environment of physical and spiritual support. Gifts are used properly and Christians find themselves mutually dependent on one another. Barnabas was a team person, one who "brought Paul into the mainstream of Christianity."[28]

*6. Flexibility.* Serving in changing communities, contextualizing into multicultural dynamics, and working with people from different socioeconomic strata require flexibility. It is one of the most difficult aspects of leadership. Young leaders need to understand that in today's world, everything is changing—except the eternal Word of God. Flexibility must be learned, appreciated and applied responsibly. Because the urban setting forces people to develop survival skills, most indigenous leaders will already be flexible to some degree. They will need to direct it toward responsible and useful ends.

*7. Visibility.* The missionary or pastor should be able to observe that God has gifted potential leaders in a visible way for the task of leading and serving. They bear some visible quality of leadership. "Leadership never translates as anything less than leadership," says Calvin Miller.[29]

Visible leadership qualities include charisma, followers, attitude, appearance, administrative ability, multifaceted personality, willingness to serve others and visionary aptitude. In any case, they can be seen.

*8. Biblical commitment.* To be an effective servant of God, a leader must exhibit biblical leadership. In urban ministry we tend to be too pragmatic with emerging leaders. Or we may give authority to Hispanic leadership prematurely. In Luke 22, the Lord has communion with his disciples. The fellowship is intimate and worshipful, and yet after the sharing, a rivalry occurs. A power-play is revealed, accusations are made, and the Lord rebukes the disciples by saying, "You are not to be like that" (22:26). We must always look for leaders who focus on God and his will as revealed in Scripture. The teaching of 1 Timothy 3 should be at the top of our list of qualifications. Leaders can make critical mistakes when they are trained without biblical criteria.

### Conclusion

In this chapter we have seen that leadership development always involves a process. We have also recognized that the context for training must be taken seriously. While local church involvement in the training process is essential, formal education as recommended by Justo González is also desirable. I agree with him that not only should education be encouraged, but *quality* education. To accept anything less "because you are Hispanics" will severely limit the students' growth. And finally, building a contextually appropriate theological framework, building relationships, building servants, and building a selection process will greatly enhance the development of second-generation leaders.

# Chapter 10

## Mentoring

A much-talked-about method of developing ministry leaders—though far from new—is that of mentoring. The practice is well entrenched in our early history of ministry training. At one time it operated like an apprenticeship in which a young leader was trained by the local pastor to serve in a new or ongoing parish. Hispanic churches historically have trained their own leaders. Mentoring often takes place without much deliberate planning. It is usually pragmatic, sensible and appropriate for the immediate need. But because effective mentoring requires a great deal of time and energy, many have not made the effort to provide new leaders with the proper tools for ministry.

If more churches practiced mentoring in a deliberate form, their new leaders would be much more effective, and the cause of Christ would be multiplied in the world. Mentoring is essential to providing the church with well-prepared leaders. It can take place in the process of church planting, church growth and leadership development. Seminaries and Bible institutes are helpful aspects of a leader's development, but they cannot be substitutes for mentoring. Mentoring is a personal undertaking by the pastor, elder, servant-leader or well-equipped layperson who will train others for effective ministry. It is pastors preparing pastors, missionaries developing missionaries, and evangelists training evangelists.

## Biblical Dimensions of Mentoring

Mentoring flows out of the reservoir of God's Word, and biblical mentoring prepares Christian leaders for service and solidarity (Eph 4:12-13). Several important biblical concepts are foundational for mentoring.

*1. Church organism.* Mentoring begins with the understanding that the church is a growing, dynamic organism with divine and contextual structure (Eph 4:15-16). Paul speaks of the church as growing up (Eph 4:15), built up (Eph 4:12), "joined and held together by every supporting ligament . . . as each part does its work" (Eph 4:16). We are speaking of a living entity. "An organism that does not grow is in reality dead."[1] The mentoring process, therefore, takes on the seriousness of being prepared and equipped to continue Christ's incarnation in the world. The church is the body of Christ (Eph 5:23), and it has been called into being by God. Too often pastors select new leaders based on their popularity and desire alone. This approach violates the Word of God. Jesus calls leaders to be his stewards (Jn 15:16). True mentoring prepares those chosen by God to enhance the growth of the church as a whole. There is no room for leaders who do not see the church as the body of Christ, a covenant people divinely called to grow.

Donald MacNair states, "The pastor is the building block of a living church. What he does and the way in which he does it has a significant bearing on the church's vitality."[2] The Antiochan church was blessed with faithful and capable leadership (Acts 13:1).

The leaders were called prophets and teachers. Their primary ministry was to equip the church in which the disciples were first called Christians (Acts 11:26). The listing of these servant-leaders reminds us of both the divine initiation of selecting and installing these men and the contextual relevancy in discharging the gospel to a diverse congregation (Acts 13:1-3).

Mentoring is influenced both by divine and contextual structure, not only by an analysis of community and world but also by an analysis of God's providence and power.

*2. Christological preparation.*

But to each one of us grace has been given as Christ apportioned it. This is why it says:

"When he ascended on high,

he led captives in his train

and gave gifts to men."

(What does "he ascended" mean except that he also descended to the lower, earthly regions? He who descended is the very one who ascended higher than all the heavens, in order to fill the whole universe.) It was he who gave some to be apostles, some to be prophets, some to be evangelists, and some to be pastors and teachers. (Eph 4:7-11)

The task of mentoring depends on Christ as the giver of grace. In the first four chapters of Ephesians, Paul communicates the astounding joy of God's grace. The sovereign election of God is announced (1:3-5), and it is this very grace that is given to the church for service (4:7-13). Christ has apportioned his grace to each member (4:7). This subjective grace works in us and finds its fruit in the church's call to world evangelization. Christ is the equipper of the church for service. To begin without dependence on Christ as the giver of grace is to become person-centered rather than Christ-centered. A willing heart is important to the process of mentoring, but it can never supersede the preparation of Christ. This raises several other points.

Our potential as God's children depends on Christ and a yielded

167

life. Christ has given grace to each as he apportioned it (4:7). Often we are too quick to judge the potential of servant-leaders based on personality traits, psychological manifestations and academic qualities rather than on God's grace. By doing this we limit the movement of God's church in the world.

Another important dimension to Christ's preparation is the selection for unique ministry of those he has called (4:11). Paul was humbled on the way to Damascus and ordered by the Lord to "get up and go into the city, and you will be told what you must do" (Acts 9:6).

> The church is thus a God-created and indwelled community. It is the body of Christ, integrated by many members with diverse functions. It is the fellowship of the Spirit, set apart for service by its grace and purifying fire.[3]

In Ephesians 4:11 the emphasis is on the giver. He himself and no other is the giver. God is the one who calls and prepares.

A mentor does not vote for someone to be a servant-leader, or decide to manipulate another for the Lord's field of service. The task of mentoring is to discover whom God has touched and anointed. Christological preparation is a theology of hope for the church. The Lord not only equips the church, but he also selects and empowers those for significant ministry in the world. It is divinely apportioned and therefore perfect and just.

*3. Christological mandate* (Eph 4:12-13). Christ has prepared us to prepare others for service. In this milieu of preparing, repairing and equipping, God has specifically recognized and called certain people to be the emerging pastor-teachers, evangelists, church planters and preachers of the Word (4:11). It is Christ's calling to prepare the church for service, unity and growth (4:12-13). The process takes time (2 Cor 3:18) and will culminate in glory (Rom 8:29-30). Mentoring concerns itself not merely with leaders, but with servant-leaders. In the New Testament leadership is viewed as service or *diakonia* (1 Cor 16:15-16; 12:28; 2 Cor 3:7-9; 4:1; 5:18; 6:3; 2 Tim 4:5; Eph 4:11-13; Col 4:17). The idea of service is a functional matter of the leader truly called by the Lord. It is what Peter exhorts the presbyter to do, to tend the flocks of God (1 Pet 5:1-4). The ruling aspect is present, but the christological mandate is to serve (1 Cor 3:5; 2 Cor 1:24). Mentoring can never be a step to higher ground—only to holy ground. Therefore, in mentoring the goal is not to equip for position but rather for function, that is, service so that the body of Christ may be built up (Eph 4:12). Mentoring others is a major responsibility of following the giver of gifts, Christ, within the church historically and culturally.

## Biblical Models

Mentoring primarily follows a New Testament model of praxis, but not exclusively. God provided mentoring for his leaders throughout Scripture. Joseph and Moses were not only Egyptianized, they were mentored in various ways by others. Jethro visited Moses; Aaron was provided as a "designated hitter" as well as a tutor for Moses; David learned from Saul, from the child playing in the courts to the king designing the temple and leading Israel. But the primary biblical teaching on mentoring comes from Jesus, Barnabas and Paul in the New Testament. "A student is not above his teacher," Jesus said, "but everyone who is fully trained will be like his teacher" (Lk 6:40).

*1. Jesus.* Jesus selected, prepared and sent those he mentored. Christ's method of choosing differs dramatically from that of major corporations or, for that matter, major denominations and churches. Corporations screen for the appropriate character and personality, the person who has all the qualities. Jesus selects the unqualified and gives them his Spirit. They were equipped not for maintenance, but rather to throw the city into an uproar (Acts 16:20), to cause trouble in the world (Acts 17:6). In Luke 5, Jesus called the first disciples to himself using a divine selection process. Those he chose did not seem particularly appropriate as servant-leaders, but Jesus knew them and therefore called them to be fishers of men. His practice was to call people first to himself and then to the world (Lk 5:10). Mentoring is not a selfish task; it is the task of calling others to do the work of ministry. It is even calling others to do greater tasks that will bear even more fruit (Jn 14:12). In Luke 5, the preparation begins with observation of Jesus' ministry; then he empowers them to carry on a similar ministry (Mt 10:1), and he sends them out (Mt 10:5). This process continued right up to the conclusion of his earthly ministry. He called them to go and make disciples because all authority was available through him (Mt 28:16-20). The disciples observed and served, and the mentoring process after Jesus' ascension continued. We see this process most clearly in the relationship between Barnabas and Paul.

*2. Barnabas.* This man became the link between Christianity and the Gentile world. As a Jewish Levite coming out of Cyprus, he would also provide flexibility within a multicultural situation. In Acts 4:36-37 we notice his willingness to be committed to the body of Christ. When Barnabas met Paul and discovered what God had already done in him, he affirmed Paul in the presence of the apostles (Acts 9:27). The mentor is usually the one who knows the individual best, and can affirm conversion, gifts and use of gifts. Colaboring is also part of the curriculum. Barnabas brought Paul to Antioch because he needed help discipling the new and growing congregation there. Barnabas was Paul's link to ministry. It was arranged by God, making it possible for Paul to observe and serve with Barnabas.

Keep in mind that Paul was mentored by a person who was good, full of the Holy Spirit and faith (Acts 11:24). Barnabas was a man of integrity, sensitive to the guidance of the Holy Spirit. He had made the effort to find Paul because he had discovered God's potential in him. Paul was mentored by a man prepared by God for this missiological task. Barnabas discovered God's selection and prepared Paul through colaboring (Acts 11:22-30; 13:1-3; 14:23; 15:1-4). This exchange of preparation ended with Paul's disagreement concerning Barnabas's decision to take Mark, and therefore new mentoring situations were established: Barnabas and Mark,

Paul and Silas. The continuation of mentoring is obvious. Paul is now sent out, but has begun to serve and mentor with another disciple (Acts 16).

*3. Paul.* Paul's model is christological. Paul does not just speak to others about growing and serving; he functions with them (1 Thess 1:1; Phil 1:1) and displays the grace apportioned him. Paul was always concerned with making an impact on others. "You know how we lived among you for your sake. You became imitators of us and of the Lord" (1 Thess 1:5-6). As a mentor, Paul entrusts the gospel to reliable men (2 Tim 2:1-2) so that the ministry may go on. Paul mentors Timothy by colaboring, observing what God is doing and then sending him to do the significant service of God.

## Biblical Principles

*1. The mentor is filled with the Holy Spirit.* Barnabas and Paul displayed a life of holiness and commitment to Christ. The modeling aspect of mentoring is extremely powerful. "Everyone who is fully trained will be like his teacher" (Lk 6:40). It is imperative that those who are mentored also become holy (1 Pet 1:16). The mentor is holy.

*2. The mentor must be active in service.* Ruling is secondary to service. Both Paul and Barnabas were active servants. While Paul was preaching in Tarsus, Barnabas found him for another task that would use his gifts (Acts 11:25-30). The point here is that we cannot mentor others from a theoretical position. Nor can we teach without practice. The mentor is a practitioner. This is important because we tend to intellectualize and avoid the actual doing of ministry. We become intellectual missionaries and evangelists and teachers without ever getting real practice. For the Christian, mentoring must be "one beggar telling another beggar where to find bread."

*3. The mentor must be flexible.* Paul was able to "shift gears" when he was called by Barnabas. Also, Paul served with an interesting and diversified group of men (Acts 13:1), which required further flexibility to have the Holy Spirit use him. And Paul eventually left with a new partner in mission, Silas (Acts 15:40). Paul was not hindered from going to Syria and Cilicia to strengthen the churches. The mission goes on when we are willing to adjust to changing circumstances. Mentoring without flexibility makes it difficult to hear God's voice in a complex world.

*4. The mentor must be passionate for service.* The accounts of Paul, Barnabas, Timothy and Peter depict men who are passionate for the gospel of Christ. Paul exhorted Timothy to fan into flame the gift of God (2 Tim 1:6). In the same context Paul encouraged his son in the faith not to be ashamed to testify about our Lord (2 Tim 1:8). The call to serve is ongoing for the mentor who is completely in love with Christ.

*5. The mentor is deeply committed to those he or she is mentoring.* Paul clearly expresses his emotional attachment to Timothy (2 Tim 1:3-4). The mentor is never so concerned about the mission that he loses perspective on the individuals Christ has given him. Barnabas and Jesus also displayed this deep concern for those God had entrusted to them.

*6. The mentor is committed for the duration of the race.* Both Paul and Barnabas were engaged in the task of mentoring until the very end. Jesus also displayed this kind of loyalty. The privilege of mentoring others for God's service is great, but the responsibilities are life-long—in sickness and in health. A temporary commitment is impossible.

*7. The mentor must be a Christian devoted to holiness.* He or she must reflect the image of God in society (1 Pet 1:13-16). This biblical principle (brought out earlier in the chapter) bears expansion. The mentor must put aside the old man with his deeds and put on the new man (Col 3:9-10; Eph 4:22-24). The same idea appears in Romans 12:2. The mentor must first follow God before he can call others to follow him. Charles Hodge describes this expression of devotion and love:

> Love to God, however, is not mere complacency in moral excel-
> lence. It is the love of a personal Being, who stands in the most

172

intimate relations to ourselves, as the Author of our existence, as our Preserver and Ruler, as our Father, who with conscious love watches over us, protects us, supplies all our wants, holds communion with us, manifesting himself unto us as he does not unto the world. The feelings of dependence, obligation, and relationship, enter largely into that comprehensive affection called the love of God. This affection is still further modified by the apprehension of the infinite wisdom and power of its object. These attributes are the proper objects of admiration; and, when infinite in degree and united with infinite goodness, they excite that wonder, admiration, reverence, and complacency, which constitute adoration, and which find in prostration and worship their only adequate expression.[4]

These moving words cause us to stop and recognize our greatest goal in life: to be conformed to the image of Christ (Rom 8:29). The mentor too often is described as someone who provides resources for ministry rather than for living. Both are essential; one without the other nullifies the whole. After years of mentoring others, I must confess that the most important and the most difficult aspect for me was the priority of holiness—to provide emerging leaders with a testimony, sanctified to God for his glory. As Hodge notes, "It is impossible that those who have correct views and feelings in regard to God should not feel and act correctly in regard to their fellow men."[5] Therefore, a mentor must devote time and practice to living righteously before the Lord.

*8. The mentor must be well prepared theologically.* The Word of God is the strength and power of biblical ministry. In many of our urban Hispanic churches, the issue is not so much the infallibility of the Word of God but the appropriation of the Word of God in context. Moisés Silva reviews the subject of contextualization:

It would be a mistake, however, to jettison the basic concept of contextualization simply because it has been abused. The fact is that every attempt we make at understanding the Bible (or any other ancient document) necessarily involves transferring a particular text from one historical context to another. When contemporary Christians read a portion of Scripture (already partially contextualized by the English version!), they can make sense of it only from the context of their own knowledge and experience.

The question, therefore, is not *whether* we should contextualize, for we all do it, but rather, *how* to do it without compromising the integrity of the Bible.[6]

Preaching too often is contextualized inappropriately, and the true meaning of the text is misunderstood. Giving in to the pressure to be relevant without using good hermeneutical skills is dangerous. We convince ourselves that our present-day concerns are the exact concerns of the biblical text. On the other hand, we must not deny our pressing issues and needs. Silva notes,

Of course, we must be very careful not to read into the text present-day concerns that are not really there, but it is proper and even necessary to approach the Bible with a strong awareness of our needs. The problems faced in the gospel ministry often alert us to truths in Scripture that might otherwise remain veiled to us. Proper exegesis consists largely of asking the right questions from the text, and the life of the church can provide us with those very questions.[7]

The need of many of our pastors is to learn how to do biblical exposition. This calls for biblical exegesis that takes into account systematic theology as well as biblical theology.

The truth is that one cannot really practice, say, biblical exegesis without taking into account the concerns of systematic theology; similarly, it would be artificial to suggest that we must not or cannot address the problems posed by practical ministry until we have fully explored the area of biblical theology.[8]

The mentor who has not developed exegetical and hermeneutical skills will find it most difficult to prepare emerging leaders to be exegetes of the Word of God. To have a prosperous and successful ministry, we must do what the the Word of God tells us (Josh 1:8).

*9. The mentor must be sociologically and anthropologically prepared.* God speaks his eternal Word to people in concrete, historical situations. If we are to proclaim the good news with the intention of seeing all of life confess Jesus Christ as Lord, then we must consider the dialogue between the Word of God and the social sciences to be important. Too often we have omitted this dialogue and overemphasized the interaction between theology and philosophy. Our major need is to understand the historical and social context in which we are ministering. The awareness of transitions and social evils provides the context in which the Word will be presented, along with the dynamics of cultural distinctions. The urban context is a complicated reality that needs serious study. In many cities the church is vulnerable because it does not understand the social dynamics or the power of God to bring reconciliation; therefore, we have white flight, black flight, and brown flight to another context much more sociologically and theologically comfortable. Mentors must be skilled in guiding emerging leaders not only through demographic work but also ethnographic documentation.

*10. The mentor must be mentored.* The one aspect so vital to fruitful mentoring is that the mentor continues to grow within a milieu of experienced and mature Christians. A good mentor is one who is being mentored.

## Clarifying the Mentor's Role

In closing this chapter, I want to give further definition to the role of the mentor, both in theory and practice. *Funk & Wagnall's New Practical Standard Dictionary*[9] defines mentor as "a wise and faithful teacher, guide and friend; an elderly monitor or adviser." This definition provides us with several implications. One is that mentors are to be mature, growing individuals who have the ability to make beneficial decisions. It is their responsibility to equip others for the purpose of living productive lives. In the biblical sense, a mentor equips others for the work of the ministry (Eph 4:11-12).

At the same time, the mentor is not to do what God intends the whole body to do. For the purpose of this book, the mentor prepares emerging leaders to do ministry in the urban context. The mentor equips them to plant churches that are faithful to God's Word and to display God's kingdom in context. The mentor teaches these emerging leaders to be productive and to model the gospel of Jesus Christ in their community. The mentor also prepares them to become mentors themselves in due time.

The mentor never leaves his responsibility (as was indicated earlier), but rather finds new and creative ways to share his wisdom as leaders grow more confident, reliable and interdependent. An example of this change is when the mentor or the emerging leader relocates. Because of geographical limitations, the mentor recognizes that his role has changed and tries to find new ways to serve. He may only be able to provide advice by writing letters or making phone calls. I know of a case where the mentor has relocated out of state and the pastor calls him to review and critique sermons. This pastor also calls his mentor for advice about congregational issues. This mentoring may seem limited, but it still provides ongoing support, instruction, and evaluation. The mentoring responsibility is sometimes likened to a parent who prepares his or her children to be productive individuals. When they are ready to leave and be on their own, the parent does not cease to be a parent; only the job description changes. The ultimate evaluation of the mentor is the reproduction of one's godliness and ministry (1 Thess 1:4-10). The emerging leaders eventually become mentors who are reproducing themselves in others in an urban context.

As we can see, the life of the mentor is dependent on the Lord God, who controls us through the Holy Spirit. The mentor must be a Christian who is not only prepared in ministry but who also walks in submission to God's will.[10]

Mentoring is the task of commitment and service to others. Paul in a dramatic way describes the agony of involvement: "I served the Lord with great humility and with tears, although I was severely tested by the plots of the Jews. You know that I have not hesitated to preach anything that would be helpful to you" (Acts 20:19-20a).

The dividends are extraordinary if we are willing to pursue a reproductive agenda, which implies presenting our lives to others as stewards of God's gospel. Hispanic leaders have always learned from observing others in their integral involvement in God's mission. The areas lacking may have been reflection and the provision, as González describes it, of academic and intellectual tools.[11] The church has always been the starting and ending point. More deliberate forms of mentoring will enhance the overall formulation of emerging leaders for effective ministry in the urban context of the United States.

Mentoring is a necessary component for developing leadership. It is not easily done. Most of us have never experienced substantial mentoring and are not sure what it looks like. But I think it warrants some investigation. Moreover, it requires our willingness to risk the attempt of overseeing emerging leaders in a deliberate and strategic manner. The biblical accounts show us how important this was in the life of the early church. It is a way of passing on valuable information and skills.

One difficult aspect of the mentoring relationship—more of a personal than a theological issue—is when one or both of the parties must depart. Too often the separation comes unexpectedly, before the mentoree and the mentor have been able to devise a sensible plan on how to move ahead independently. Conflict frequently results. Yet the interesting thing is that the relationship eventually comes back together once the mentoree has built a certain amount of confidence.

# Conclusion

In the process of researching this material, I was privileged to encounter a wealth of Hispanic authors who were both enriching and encouraging toward the pursuit of excellence. The ability of these authors to go beyond the boundaries of research and reflect critically on both the text and context was an eye-opener for me. The uniqueness of style and communication was encouraging. One such author and friend is the late Dr. Orlando Costas. He was an extraordinary individual who challenged all who would dare engage in the missiological task of doing theology in context. He moved us into theological and biblical discovery as he profoundly aroused our mission hearts.

The ongoing dialogue between Roman Catholic and Protestant theologians provides a new frontier for doing theology and apologetics among evangelicals. I am still awaiting the kind of theological discussion on issues that will provoke the Roman Catholic and Protestant church to search deeper into the biblical text.

Education stands out as a necessary requirement for leadership development. We are still falling short of the mark. "In 1985-86, only four Hispanics completed Ph.D.'s, Th.D.'s, or S.T.D.'s."[1] I am sure some practitioners will argue with me about this. They might say that what we need are more church planters and evangelists. I would not argue the need for growth, but if we are to face the future realistically and provide the kind of scholarship that will motivate and set an example for emerging leaders, we must take the academic field seriously as a mission in the U.S.

The Hispanic church must come to grips with the loss of its second-generation young people and find creative ways to allow them to embrace an attainable vision of the church.

The bilingual issues in the church must become part of the agenda for growth. I often get mail from Hispanic faculty members of other institutions who are seeking to gather professors for dialogue and research. The first thought that comes to mind is, What will happen to those who are not necessarily competent in Spanish? Yet all of the mail I have ever received has been in Spanish, which also means the discussion is totally in one language. We should not exclude the Spanish language, but we must provide avenues for others to enter into the dialogue with their language limitations. For many, two years of high-school Spanish is all they have had. How should we bridge the cultural gap? Marginalization will occur within the subgroups. If we are to talk of Hispanic theology in the U.S., we must integrate the second- and third-generation experience.

The demographics provided in this volume present a missiological challenge not only for crosscultural ministry, but also for the Hispanic church and its growing second generation. The Hispanic church and its rich heritage of mission and passion for the lost must be passed down to our children. We are in need of each other. Youth must know their past and present in order to better understand their future.

# APPENDIX

## Supplemental Tables for Chapter One

### Table A1: Occupation by U.S. Subgroup, 1990

| Occupation | Total Pop. Male | Fem. | Hispanics Male | Fem. | Non-Hispanics Male | Fem. |
|---|---|---|---|---|---|---|
| **White-Collar Workers** | | | | | | |
| Managerial and Professional Specialty | 26.3 | 27.2 | 11.4 | 15.8 | 27.6 | 28.0 |
| Technical, Sales, and Administrative Support | 20.5 | 44.1 | 15.1 | 39.8 | 21.0 | 44.3 |
| Service Occupations | 10.4 | 17.6 | 17.1 | 26.2 | 9.8 | 17.0 |
| Farming, Forestry, and Fishing | 4.1 | .9 | 8.6 | 1.2 | 3.7 | .9 |
| **Blue-Collar Workers** | | | | | | |
| Precision Production, Craft and Repair | 18.8 | 2.2 | 18.7 | 3.0 | 18.8 | 2.1 |
| Operators, Fabricators, and Laborers | 19.9 | 8.1 | 29.1 | 14.0 | 19.1 | 7.6 |

Source: U.S. Bureau of the Census, Current Population Reports, Series P-20, No. 455, *The Hispanic Population in the United States: March 1991* (Washington, D.C.: U.S. Government Printing Office), p. 12.

## Table A2: Average Dropout Rate by Hispanic Subgroup, 1980

| Subgroup | Native-Born | Foreign-Born |
|---|---|---|
| Mexican | 30.4 | 59.4 |
| Puerto Rican | 31.9 | 47.2 |
| Cuban | 11.4 | 16.1 |
| Central/South American | 4.5 | 18.3 |
| Other Hispanic | 7.3 | 24.5 |

Source: Frank D. Bean and Marta Tienda, *The Hispanic Population of the United States* (New York: Russell Sage Foundation, 1987), pp. 272-73.

## Table A3: Dissimilarities and Contact Probabilities Between Selected Hispanic Groups and Anglos, 1980

| City | Hispanic-Anglo Dissimilarity | | | Probability of Contact Between Hispanic Group and Anglos | | |
|---|---|---|---|---|---|---|
| | Mex. | P.R. | Cuban | Mex. | P.R. | Cuban |
| Los Angeles | .611 | .538 | .596 | .320 | .445 | .489 |
| New York | .660 | .723 | .597 | .433 | .278 | .510 |
| Miami | .562 | .441 | .588 | .467 | .393 | .311 |
| Chicago | .640 | .805 | .671 | .486 | .450 | .690 |
| San Antonio | .589 | .517 | .582 | .272 | .548 | .606 |

Source: Frank D. Bean and Marta Tienda, *The Hispanic Population of the United States* (New York: Russell Sage Foundation, 1987), p. 174.

# Notes

## Introduction

[1] Hispanic Policy Development Project, *The Hispanic Almanac* (New York: Hispanic Policy Development Project, 1984), p. 27.

[2] Justo González, *Mañana: Christian Theology from a Hispanic Perspective* (Nashville: Abingdon, 1990), p. 53.

## Chapter One: Urbanization: The Hispanic Reality

[1] Isidro Lucas, *Aquí Estamos* (Chicago: Chicago United, 1978), pp. 1-2.

[2] The Latino National Political Survey conducted in 1989-90 as reported in "Datanote on the Puerto Rican Community," *Institute for Puerto Rican Policy* 13 (April 1993): 2.

[3] Felix Padilla, *Latino Ethnic Consciousness: The Case of Mexican Americans and Puerto Ricans in Chicago* (Notre Dame, Ind.: University of Notre Dame Press, 1985), p. 3.

[4] Ibid.

[5] Joane Nagel and Susan Olzak, "Ethnic Mobilization in New and Old States: An Extension of the Competition Model," *Social Problems* 30 (1982): 132.

[6] Lucas, *Aquí Estamos*, p. 3.

[7] Isidro Lucas, *The Browning of America: The Hispanic Revolution in the American Church* (Chicago: Fides Claretian, 1981), pp. 5-6.

[8] Antonio M. Stevens Arroyo, ed., *Prophets Denied Honor: An Anthology on the Hispanic Church in the United States* (Maryknoll, N.Y.: Orbis Press, 1980), p. 1.

[9] In Hispanic literature the terms *white* and *Anglo* are both used when referring to the U.S. majority population. This book will use both terms, but not interchangeably. When speaking statistically, especially when using census data, the terms *white* or *non-Hispanic white* are used because they relate to census-defined racial categories. However, when speaking culturally, the term *Anglo* is preferred.

[10] Lucas, *Aquí Estamos*, p. 3.

[11] Raymond Rivera, "The Hispanic Context in the United States," in *The Gospel and Urbanization*, ed. Robert T. Coote (Ventnor, N.J.: Overseas Ministries Study Center, 1985), p. 73.

[12] Justo L. González, *The Theological Education of Hispanics* (New York: Fund for Theological Education, 1988), p. 11.

[13] Rivera, "The Hispanic Context," p. 73.

[14] Ibid.

[15]U.S. Bureau of the Census, Current Population Reports, Series P-20, No. 455, *The Hispanic Population in the United States: March 1991* (Washington, D.C.: U.S. Government Printing Office), p. 10.

[16]Ibid., pp. 18-19.

[17]Ibid., p. 18.

[18]Ibid., p. 13.

[19]Ibid., p. 12.

[20]Marta Tienda, "Nationality and Income Attainment Among Native and Immigrant Hispanic Men in the United States," *The Sociological Quarterly* 24 (Spring 1983): 270.

[21]U.S. Bureau of the Census, *The Hispanic Population,* p. 10.

[22]Janice Petrovich, *Northeast Hispanic Needs: A Guide for Action* (Washington, D.C.: ASPIRA Association, 1987), 1:xv.

[23]Ibid.

[24]Hispanic Policy Development Project, *The Hispanic Almanac* (New York: Hispanic Policy Development Project, 1987), p. 31.

[25]Clara Rodríguez, *Puerto Ricans Born in the U.S.A.* (Boston: Unwin Hyman, 1989), p. 69.

[26]Frank D. Bean and Marta Tienda, *The Hispanic Population of the United States* (New York: Russell Sage Foundation, 1987), p. 171.

[27]Ibid., p. 177.

[28]Petrovich, *Northeast Hispanic Needs,* 2:34.

## Chapter Two: A Historical Exchange

[1]L. H. Gann and Peter J. Duignan, *The Hispanics in the United States: A History* (Boulder, Colo.: Westview Press, 1986), p. 3.

[2]Ibid.

[3]Ibid.

[4]Ellwyn Stoddard, *Mexican Americans: Ethnic Groups in Comparative Perspective* (New York: Random House, 1973), p. 4.

[5]Justo González, *Mañana: Christian Theology from a Hispanic Perspective* (Nashville: Abingdon, 1990), p. 31.

[6]Earl Shorris, *Latinos: A Biography of the People* (New York: Norton, 1992), p. 95.

[7]Stoddard, *Mexican Americans,* p. 9.

[8]Gann and Duignan, *Hispanics in the United States,* p. 6.

[9]Ibid., p. 14.

[10]González, *Mañana,* p. 32.

[11]Justo González, *The Theological Education of Hispanics* (New York: Fund for Theological Education, 1988), pp. 20-21.

[12]Stoddard, *Mexican Americans,* p. 14.

[13]Wayne MoQuin, ed., *A Documentary History of the Mexican Americans* (New York: Praeger Publishing, 1971), p. 120.

[14]Gann and Duignan, *Hispanics in the United States,* p. 37.

[15]Ibid., p. 41.

[16]Paul S. Taylor, *Mexican Labor in the United States* (Berkeley: University of California Press, 1932), 2:275, as quoted in Gann and Duignan, *Hispanics in the United*

*States*, p. 44.

[17] Leobardo F. Estrada, F. Chris García, Reynaldo Flores Macías and Lionel Maldonado, "Chicanos in the United States: A History of Exploitation and Resistance," *Daedalus* 110, no. 2 (1981): 117.

[18] Douglas Massey, "The Social Organization of Mexican Migration to the United States," *The Annals of the American Academy of Political and Social Science* 487 (1986): 111.

[19] Ibid., pp. 107-8.

[20] Antonio M. Stevens Arroyo and Virgilio Elizondo, "The Spanish-Speaking in the United States," in *Prophets Denied Honor: An Anthology on the Hispanic Church in the United States*, ed. Antonio M. Stevens Arroyo (Maryknoll, N.Y.: Orbis Press, 1980), p. 12.

[21] Clara Rodríguez, *Puerto Ricans Born in the U.S.A.* (Boston: Unwin Hyman, 1989), p. 1.

[22] Ibid., p. 10.

[23] Ibid., p. 4.

[24] Ibid., p. 49.

[25] Ibid., p. 19.

[26] Gerald Eugene Poyo, *With All, and for the Good of All: The Emergence of Popular Nationalism in the Cuban Communities of the United States* (Durham, N.C.: Duke University Press, 1989), p. 1.

[27] Ibid., p. 5.

[28] Ibid., p. 52.

[29] Ibid., p. 53.

[30] Thomas D. Boswell and James R. Curtis, *The Cuban-American Experience: Culture, Images and Perspectives* (Totowa, N.J.: Rowman and Allanheld, 1983), p. 15.

[31] Shorris, *Latinos*, p. 41.

[32] Gann and Duignan, *Hispanics in the United States*, p. 94.

[33] Boswell and Curtis, *Cuban-American Experience*, p. 11.

[34] Gann and Duignan, *Hispanics in the United States*, p. 103.

[35] Boswell and Curtis, *Cuban-American Experience*, p. 1.

[36] Ibid., p. 174.

[37] Ibid., p. 183.

[38] Gann and Duignan, *Hispanics in the United States*, p. 103.

[39] Emilio A. Núñez C. and William D. Taylor, *Crisis in Latin America: An Evangelical Perspective* (Chicago: Moody Press, 1989).

[40] Gann and Duignan, *Hispanics in the United States*, p. 113.

[41] Ibid., p. 115.

## Chapter Three: Hispanic People in a New Context

[1] Antonio M. Stevens Arroyo, "Caribbean Unity," in *Prophets Denied Honor: An Anthology on the Hispanic Church in the United States*, ed. Antonio M. Stevens Arroyo (Maryknoll, N.Y.: Orbis Press, 1980), p. 14.

[2] Ibid.

[3] Richard Rodriguez, *Hunger of Memory: The Education of Richard Rodriguez* (New York: Bantam Books, 1982).

[4] Ibid., p. 22.

[5] Ibid., pp. 28-29.

[6] Ibid., p. 32.

[7] Ibid.

[8] Ibid., p. 45.

[9] Manuel A. Machado Jr., *Listen Chicano! An Informal History of the Mexican American* (Chicago: Nelson Hall, 1978), p. 133.

[10] Ibid.

[11] Hispanic Policy Development Project, *The Hispanic Almanac* (New York: Hispanic Policy Development Project, 1984), p. 39.

[12] Samuel Betances and Ricardo R. Fernández, "Political Status of Puerto Rico, 1975: Can the Legitimacy of the 'Free Associated State' Be Salvaged?" *The Rican: Journal of Contemporary Puerto Rican Thought* 2, no. 2-3, pp. 28-29.

[13] Manuel Maldonado-Denis, *Puerto Rico: A Socio-Historic Interpretation* (New York: Vintage, 1971), p. 67.

[14] Isidro Lucas, *The Browning of America: The Hispanic Revolution in the American Church* (Chicago: Fides Claretian, 1981), p. 14.

[15] Antonio M. Stevens Arroyo and Virgilio P. Elizondo, "The Spanish-Speaking in the United States," in *Prophets Denied Honor,* ed. Arroyo, p. 12.

[16] Hispanic Policy Development Project, *The Hispanic Almanac,* p. 43.

[17] Felix Padilla, *Latino Ethnic Consciousness: The Case of Mexican Americans and Puerto Ricans in Chicago* (Notre Dame, Ind.: University of Notre Dame Press, 1985), p. 39.

[18] Clara E. Rodríguez, Virginia Sánchez Korrol and José Oscar Alers, "The Puerto Rican Struggle to Survive in the United States," in *The Puerto Rican Struggle: Essays on Survival in the U.S.,* ed. Clara E. Rodríguez, Virginia Sánchez Korrol and José Oscar Alers (Maplewood, N.J.: Waterfront Press, 1980), p. 2.

[19] Ibid.

[20] Justo González, *The Theological Education of Hispanics* (New York: Fund for Theological Education, 1988), p. 28.

[21] Ibid.

[22] Arroyo and Elizondo, "Spanish-Speaking in the United States," p. 7.

[23] Ibid., p. 8.

[24] Miguel Montiel, "Chicanos in the United States: An Overview of Socio-Historical Context and Emerging Perspectives," in *Hispanic Families: Critical Issues for Policy and Programs in Human Services,* ed. Miguel Montiel (Washington, D.C.: National Coalition of Hispanic Mental Health and Human Services Organizations, 1978), p. 19.

[25] Ibid.

[26] Manuel Maldonado-Denis, "Neo-Rican? No! Puerto Ricans!" in *Prophets Denied Honor,* ed. Arroyo, p. 261.

[27] M. Estellie Smith, "The Spanish-Speaking Population of Florida," in *Latinos in the United States,* ed. Carlos E. Cortes (New York: Arno Press, 1980), p. 120.

[28] Edna Acosta-Belén, "On the Nature of 'Spanglish,'" *The Rican: Journal of Contemporary Puerto Rican Thought* 2, no. 2-3, p. 9.

[29] Ibid., p. 7.

[30]Ibid., p. 9.
[31]Einar Haugen, *The Norwegian Language in America* (Bloomington: Indiana University Press, 1969), pp. 76-77. Cited in Acosta-Belén, "Spanglish," p. 8.
[32]Acosta-Belén, "Spanglish," pp. 10-11.
[33]Ibid., p. 11.
[34]Ibid., p. 12.
[35]Ibid., p. 9.
[36]Ibid.
[37]Ibid., p. 10.

## Chapter Four: Protestant-Roman Catholic Dialogue
[1]Ronald Takaki, ed., *From Different Shores: Perspectives on Race and Ethnicity in America* (New York: Oxford University Press, 1987), p. 5.
[2]Rodolfo O. de la Garza, ed., *Ignored Voices: Public Opinion Polls and the Latino Community* (Austin, Tex.: Center for Mexican American Studies, University of Texas at Austin, 1987), p. 2.
[3]Thomas Weyr, *Hispanics USA: Breaking the Melting Pot* (New York: Harper & Row, 1988), p. 51.
[4]Jerry L. Appleby, *Missions Have Come Home to America: The Church's Cross-Cultural Ministry to Ethnics* (Kansas City, Mo.: Beacon Hill Press, 1986), p. 23.
[5]William A. Dyrness, *Invitation to Cross-Cultural Theology: Case Studies in Vernacular Theologies* (Grand Rapids, Mich.: Zondervan, 1992), p. 14.
[6]Roberto S. Goizueta, "United Sates Hispanic Theology and the Challenge of Pluralism," in *Frontiers of Hispanic Theology in the United States,* ed. Allan Figueroa Deck (Maryknoll, N.Y.: Orbis Books, 1992), p. 1.
[7]Ibid.
[8]Allan Figueroa Deck, introduction to *Frontiers of Hispanic Theology,* ed. Deck, p. xvi.
[9]Dyrness, *Cross-Cultural Theology,* p. 24.
[10]Justo L. González, *Mañana: Christian Theology from a Hispanic Perspective* (Nashville: Abingdon Press, 1990), p. 55.
[11]David Martin, "The Hidden Fire," interview by Tim Stafford, *Christianity Today,* May 14, 1990, p. 25.
[12]González, *Mañana,* p. 63.
[13]Ellwyn Stoddard, *Mexican Americans: Ethnic Groups in Comparative Perspective* (New York: Random House, 1973), p. 96.
[14]Thomas D. Boswell and James R. Curtis, *The Cuban-American Experience: Culture, Images and Perspectives* (Totowa, N.J.: Rowman and Allanheld, 1983), p. 126.
[15]Ibid.
[16]Ibid., p. 125.
[17]Martin, "Hidden Fire," p. 26.
[18]Goizueta, "United States Hispanic Theology," p. 6.
[19]Ibid.
[20]González, *Mañana,* p. 64.
[21]Ibid., p. 67.
[22]Ibid., p. 68.

[23]Ibid., p. 69.

[24]C. Peter Wagner, foreword to *Spreading the Flame: Charismatic Churches and Missions Today*, ed. Edward K. Pousson (Grand Rapids, Mich.: Zondervan, 1992), p. 13.

[25]Virgilio Elizondo, foreword to González, *Mañana*, pp. 12-13.

## Chapter Five: The Poor and Justice

[1]Edward K. Pousson, ed., *Spreading the Flame: Charismatic Churches and Missions Today* (Grand Rapids, Mich.: Zondervan, 1992), p. 47.

[2]Ibid., p. 48.

[3]Eldin Villafañe, *The Liberating Spirit: Toward An Hispanic American Pentecostal Social Ethic* (New York: University Press of America, 1992), p. 105.

[4]David Wilkerson, *David Wilkerson Speaks Out* (Minneapolis: Bethany Fellowship, 1973), p. 15; quoted in Pousson, *Spreading the Flame*, p. 34.

[5]Villafañe, *Liberating Spirit*, p. 99.

[6]C. Peter Wagner, *Church Planting for a Greater Harvest* (Ventura, Calif.: Regal, 1990), p. 78.

[7]Viv Grigg, *Cry of the Urban Poor* (Monrovia, Calif.: MARC Publications, 1992), p. 10.

[8]Ibid.

[9]John Ronsvalle and Sylvia Ronsvalle, *The Poor Have Faces: Loving Your Neighbor in the 21st Century* (Grand Rapids, Mich.: Baker, 1992), p. 35.

[10]Orlando E. Costas, *Christ Outside the Gate: Mission Beyond Christendom* (Maryknoll, N.Y.: Orbis Books, 1982), p. 193.

[11]Ibid., p. 194.

## Chapter Six: Reconciliation

[1]Samuel Betances, "The Prejudice of Having No Prejudice in Puerto Rico," *The Rican: A Journal of Contemporary Puerto Rican Thought*, no. 2 (Winter 1972), p. 41.

[2]Ibid., p. 47.

[3]Linda Chavez, "Rainbow Collision," *The New Republic*, November 19, 1990, p. 14.

[4]Ibid.

[5]Ibid., p. 15.

[6]William A. Henry III, "Beyond the Melting Pot," *Time*, April 9, 1990, p. 28.

[7]Justo L. González, *Mañana: Christian Theology from a Hispanic Perspective* (Nashville: Abingdon, 1990), p. 36.

[8]Ibid.

[9]Orlando E. Costas, *Christ Outside the Gate: Mission Beyond Christendom* (Maryknoll, N.Y.: Orbis Books, 1982), p. 23.

[10]Ibid., p. 29.

[11]Ibid., p. 33.

## Chapter Seven: Ecclesiastical Structure

[1]Manuel Ortiz, "A Church in Missiological Tension," *Urban Mission*, September 1984, pp. 15-16.

[2]Moisés Silva, *Has the Church Misread the Bible? The History of Interpretation in the*

*Light of Current Issues* (Grand Rapids, Mich.: Zondervan, 1987), p. 23.

[3] Orlando E. Costas, *Liberating News: A Theology of Contextual Evangelization* (Grand Rapids, Mich.: Eerdmans, 1989), p. 22.

[4] Ibid., p. 20.

## Chapter Eight: Issues in Leadership Training

[1] Alvaro L. Nieves, "The Minority Experience in Evangelical Colleges," in *Ethnic Minorities and Evangelical Christian Colleges*, ed. D. John Lee, Alvaro L. Nieves and Henry L. Allen (New York: University Press of America, 1991), pp. 47-48.

[2] Justo L. González, *The Theological Education of Hispanics* (New York: Fund for Theological Education, 1988), p. 69.

## Chapter Nine: Leadership Development

[1] Justo L. González, *The Theological Education of Hispanics* (New York: Fund for Theological Education, 1988), p. 68.

[2] Ibid., p. 79.

[3] Allan Figueroa Deck, ed., *Frontiers of Hispanic Theology in the United States* (Maryknoll, N.Y.: Orbis Books, 1992), p. ix.

[4] Emilio A. Núñez C. and William D. Taylor, *Crisis in Latin America: An Evangelical Perspective* (Chicago: Moody Press, 1989), p. 319.

[5] Harvie M. Conn, *Eternal Word and Changing Worlds: Theology, Anthropology and Mission in Trialogue* (Grand Rapids, Mich.: Zondervan, 1984), p. 215.

[6] Núñez and Taylor, *Crisis in Latin America,* pp. 321-22.

[7] David J. Hesselgrave and Edward Rommen, *Contextualization: Meanings, Methods and Models* (Grand Rapids, Mich.: Baker, 1989), p. 203.

[8] Dean S. Gilliland, "Contextual Theology as Incarnational Mission," in *The Word Among Us: Contextualizing Theology for Mission Today*, ed. Dean S. Gilliland (Dallas: Word, 1989), p. 13.

[9] Ibid.

[10] González, *Theological Education*, p. 69.

[11] Ibid.

[12] Vinay Samuel and Chris Sugden, "Agenda for Missions in the Eighties and Nineties: A Discussion Starter," in *New Frontiers in Mission*, ed. Patrick Sookhdeo (Grand Rapids, Mich.: Baker, 1987), p. 62.

[13] Myron D. Rush, *Richer Relationships: How to Be a Conflict-Solver and a Friend-Winner* (Wheaton, Ill.: Victor Books, 1983), p. 163.

[14] Paulo Freire, *Pedagogy of the Oppressed,* trans. Myra Bergman Ramos (New York: Continuum, 1989), p. 59.

[15] Rush, *Richer Relationships*, p. 163.

[16] Ibid., p. 164.

[17] Ibid., pp. 166-69.

[18] Ibid., p. 171.

[19] James P. Spradley, *Participant Observation* (Fort Worth, Tex.: Holt, Rinehart and Winston, 1980), p. 56.

[20] George G. Hunter III, *The Contagious Congregation: Frontiers in Evangelism and Church Growth* (Nashville: Abingdon, 1979), pp. 41-42.

[21]Freire, *Pedagogy,* p. 57.

[22]Ibid., p. 58.

[23]González, *Theological Education,* p. 79.

[24]Roland Allen, *Missionary Methods: St Paul's or Ours?* (London: World Dominion Press, 1960), p. 111.

[25]Laura Raab and Bobby Clinton, *Barnabas—Encouraging Exhorter: A Study in Mentoring* (Altadena, Calif.: Barnabas Resources, 1985), p. 23.

[26]González, *Theological Education,* pp. 11-12.

[27]Martin Marty, *The Pro and Con Book of Religious America: A Bicentennial Argument* (Waco, Tex.: Word, 1975), p. 84.

[28]Raab and Clinton, *Barnabas,* p. 23.

[29]Calvin Miller, *Leadership* (Colorado Springs, Colo.: NavPress, 1987), p. 14.

### Chapter Ten: Mentoring

[1]Orlando E. Costas, "A Wholistic Concept of Church Growth," in *Exploring Church Growth,* ed. Wilbert R. Shenk (Grand Rapids, Mich.: Eerdmans, 1983), p. 97.

[2]Donald J. MacNair, *The Living Church: A Guide For Revitalization* (Philadelphia: Great Commission Publications, 1978), p. 43.

[3]Orlando E. Costas, "The Mission of Ministry," *Missiology* 14 (1986): 463.

[4]Charles Hodge, *The Way of Life* (Fort Washington, Pa.: Banner of Truth, 1959), pp. 211-12.

[5]Ibid., p. 214.

[6]Moisés Silva, *Has the Church Misread the Bible? The History of Interpretation in the Light of Current Issues* (Grand Rapids, Mich.: Zondervan, 1987), p. 100.

[7]Ibid., p. 22.

[8]Ibid., p. 21.

[9]Charles Earle Funk, ed., *Funk & Wagnall's New Practical Standard Dictionary* (New York: Funk & Wagnall's, 1956), p. 833.

[10]Philip Amerson's "The Role of the Mentor in Urban Ministry" and Laura Raab and Bobby Clinton's *Barnabas—Encouraging Exhorter* have also laid out a number of characteristics of a mentor which may be helpful to review. Both of these works are excellent resources on mentoring.

[11]Justo L. González, *The Theological Education of Hispanics* (New York: Fund for Theological Education, 1988), p. 79.

### Conclusion

[1]Justo L. González, *The Theological Education of Hispanics* (New York: Fund for Theological Education, 1988), p. 74.

# Bibliography

Acosta-Belén, Edna. "On the Nature of 'Spanglish.'" *The Rican: Journal of Contemporary Puerto Rican Thought* 2, no. 2-3 (1972): 7-13.

Allen, Roland. *Missionary Methods: St Paul's or Ours?* London: World Dominion Press, 1960.

Amerson, Philip. "The Role of the Mentor in Urban Ministry." In *The Gospel and Urbanization*, ed. Robert T. Coote, pp. 39-40. Ventnor, N.J.: Overseas Ministries Study Center, 1985.

Appleby, Jerry L. *Missions Have Come Home to America: The Church's Cross-Cultural Ministry to Ethnics.* Kansas City, Mo.: Beacon Hill Press, 1986.

Arroyo, Antonio M. Stevens, ed. *Prophets Denied Honor: An Anthology on the Hispanic Church in the United States.* Maryknoll, N.Y.: Orbis Press, 1980.

Bean, Frank D., and Marta Tienda. *The Hispanic Population of the United States.* New York: Russell Sage Foundation, 1987.

Betances, Samuel. "The Prejudice of Having No Prejudice in Puerto Rico." *The Rican: A Journal of Contemporary Puerto Rican Thought* 2 (Winter 1972): 41-54.

Betances, Samuel, and Ricardo R. Fernández. "Political Status of Puerto Rico, 1975: Can the Legitimacy of the 'Free Associated State' Be Salvaged?" *The Rican: Journal of Contemporary Puerto Rican Thought* 2, no. 2-3 (1972): 28-35.

Boswell, Thomas D., and James R. Curtis. *The Cuban-American Experience: Culture, Images and Perspectives.* Totowa, N.J.: Rowman and Allanheld, 1983.

Chavez, Linda. "Rainbow Collision." *The New Republic,* November 19, 1990, pp. 14-16.

Conn, Harvie M. *Eternal Word and Changing Worlds: Theology, Anthropology and Mission in Trialogue.* Grand Rapids, Mich.: Zondervan, 1984.

Costas, Orlando E. *Christ Outside the Gate: Mission Beyond Christendom.* Maryknoll, N.Y.: Orbis Books, 1982.

_____. *Liberating News: A Theology of Contextual Evangelization.* Grand Rapids, Mich.: Eerdmans, 1989.

_____. "The Mission of Ministry." *Missiology* 14 (1986): 463-72.

_____. "A Wholistic Concept of Church Growth." In *Exploring Church Growth,* ed. Wilbert R. Shenk, pp. 95-107. Grand Rapids, Mich.: Eerdmans, 1983.

De la Garza, Rodolfo O., ed. *Ignored Voices: Public Opinion Polls and the Latino Community.* Austin, Tex.: Center for Mexican American Studies, University of Texas at Austin, 1987.

"Datanote on the Puerto Rican Community." *Institute for Puerto Rican Policy* 13 (April 1993).

Deck, Allan Figueroa, ed. *Frontiers of Hispanic Theology in the United States.* Maryknoll, N.Y.: Orbis Books, 1992.

Dyrness, William A. *Invitation to Cross-Cultural Theology: Case Studies in Vernacular Theologies.* Grand Rapids, Mich.: Zondervan, 1992.

Estrada, Leobardo F., F. Chris García, Reynaldo Flores Macías and Lionel Maldonado. "Chicanos in the United States: A History of Exploitation and Resistance." *Daedalus* 110, no. 2 (1981): 103-31.

Freire, Paulo. *Pedagogy of the Oppressed.* Translated by Myra Bergman Ramos. New York: Continuum, 1989.

Gann, L. H., and Peter J. Duignan. *The Hispanics in the United States: A History.* Boulder, Colo.: Westview Press, 1986.

Gilliland, Dean S. "Contextual Theology as Incarnational Mission." In *The Word Among Us: Contextualizing Theology for Mission Today,* ed. Dean S. Gilliland, pp. 9-13. Dallas: Word, 1989.

González, Justo L. *Mañana: Christian Theology from a Hispanic Perspective.* Nashville: Abingdon, 1990.

_____. *The Theological Education of Hispanics.* New York: Fund for Theological Education, 1988.

Grigg, Viv. *Cry of the Urban Poor.* Monrovia, Calif.: MARC Publications, 1992.

Henry, William A. III. "Beyond the Melting Pot." *Time,* April 9, 1990, pp. 28-31.

Hesselgrave, David J., and Edward Rommen. *Contextualization: Meanings, Methods and Models.* Grand Rapids, Mich.: Baker, 1989.

Hispanic Policy Development Project. *The Hispanic Almanac.* New York: Hispanic Policy Development Project, 1984.

Hodge, Charles. *The Way of Life.* Fort Washington, Penn.: Banner of Truth, 1959.

Hunter, George G., III. *The Contagious Congregation: Frontiers in Evangelism and Church Growth.* Nashville: Abingdon, 1979.

Lucas, Isidro. *Aquí Estamos.* Chicago: Chicago United, 1978.

_____. *The Browning of America: The Hispanic Revolution in the American Church.* Chicago: Fides Claretian, 1981.

Machado, Manuel A., Jr. *Listen Chicano! An Informal History of the Mexican American.* Chicago: Nelson Hall, 1978.

MacNair, Donald J. *The Living Church: A Guide for Revitalization.* Philadelphia: Great Commission Publications, 1978.

Maldonado-Denis, Manuel. *Puerto Rico: A Socio-Historic Interpretation.* New York: Vintage, 1971.

Martin, David. "The Hidden Fire." Interview by Tim Stafford. *Christianity Today,* May 14, 1990, pp. 23-26.

Marty, Martin. *The Pro and Con Book of Religious America: A Bicentennial Argument.* Waco, Tex.: Word, 1975.

Massey, Douglas S. "The Social Organization of Mexican Migration to the United States." *The Annals of the American Academy of Political and Social Science* 487 (1986): 102-13.

Miller, Calvin. *Leadership.* Colorado Springs, Colo.: NavPress, 1987.

Montiel, Miguel, ed. *Hispanic Families: Critical Issues for Policy and Programs in Human Services.* Washington, D.C.: National Coalition of Hispanic Mental Health and Human Services Organization, 1978.

MoQuin, Wayne, ed. *A Documentary History of the Mexican Americans.* New York: Praeger Publishing, 1971.

Nagel, Joane, and Susan Olzak. "Ethnic Mobilization in New and Old States: An Extension of the Competition Model." *Social Problems* 30, no. 2 (1982): 127-43.

Nieves, Alvaro L. "The Minority Experience in Evangelical Colleges." In *Ethnic Minorities and Evangelical Christian Colleges,* ed. D. John Lee, Alvaro L. Nieves and Henry L. Allen, pp. 47-63. New York: University Press of America, 1991.

Núñez, Emilio C., and William D. Taylor. *Crisis in Latin America: An Evangelical Perspective.* Chicago: Moody Press, 1989.

Ortiz, Manuel. "A Church in Missiological Tension." *Urban Mission,* September 1984, pp. 12-19.

Padilla, Felix. *Latino Ethnic Consciousness: The Case of Mexican Americans and Puerto Ricans in Chicago.* Notre Dame, Ind.: University of Notre Dame Press, 1985.

Petrovich, Janice. *Northeast Hispanic Needs: A Guide for Action.* Washington, D.C.: ASPIRA Association, 1987.

Pousson, Edward K. *Spreading the Flame: Charismatic Churches and Missions Today.* Grand Rapids, Mich.: Zondervan, 1992.

Poyo, Gerald Eugene. *With All and for the Good of All: The Emergence of Popular Nationalism in the Cuban Communities of the United States.* Durham, N.C.: Duke University Press, 1989.

Raab, Laura, and Bobby Clinton. *Barnabas—Encouraging Exhorter: A Study in Mentoring.* Altadena, Calif.: Barnabas Resources, 1985.

Rivera, Luis N. *A Violent Evangelism: The Political and Religious Conquest of the Americas.* Translated by Marina Herrera. Louisville, Ky.: Westminster/John Knox Press, 1992.

Rivera, Raymond. "The Hispanic Context in the United States." In *The Gospel and Urbanization,* ed. Robert T. Coote, p. 73. Ventnor, N.J.: Overseas Ministries Study Center, 1985.

Rodríguez, Clara E. *Puerto Ricans Born in the U.S.A.* Boston: Unwin Hyman, 1989.

Rodríguez, Clara E., Virginia Sánchez Korrol and José Oscar Alers. *The Puerto Rican Struggle: Essays on Survival in the U.S.* Maplewood, N.J.: Waterfront Press, 1980.

Rodriguez, Richard. *Hunger of Memory: The Education of Richard Rodriguez.* New York: Bantam, 1982.

Ronsvalle, John, and Sylvia Ronsvalle. *The Poor Have Faces: Loving Your Neighbor in the 21st Century.* Grand Rapids, Mich.: Baker, 1992.

Rush, Myron D. *Richer Relationships: How to Be a Conflict-Solver and a Friend-Winner.* Wheaton, Ill.: Victor Books, 1983.

Samuel, Vinay, and Chris Sugden. "Agenda for Missions in the Eighties and Nineties: A Discussion Starter." In *New Frontiers in Mission,* ed. Patrick Sookhdeo, pp. 61-70. Grand Rapids, Mich.: Baker, 1987.

Shorris, Earl. *Latinos: A Biography of the People.* New York: Norton, 1992.

Silva, Moisés. *Has the Church Misread the Bible? The History of Interpretation in the Light of Current Issues.* Grand Rapids, Mich.: Zondervan, 1987.

Smith, M. Estellie. "The Spanish-Speaking Population of Florida." In *Latinos in the United States,* ed. Carlos E. Cortes, pp. 120-33. New York: Arno Press, 1980.

Spradley, James P. *Participant Observation.* Fort Worth, Tex.: Holt, Rinehart and Winston, 1980.

Stoddard, Ellwyn. *Mexican Americans: Ethnic Groups in Comparative Perspective.* New York: Random House, 1973.

Takaki, Ronald, ed. *From Different Shores: Perspectives on Race and Ethnicity in America.* New York: Oxford University Press, 1987.

Tienda, Marta. "Nationality and Income Attainment Among Native and Immigrant Hispanic Men in the United States." *The Sociological Quarterly* 24 (Spring 1983): 253-72.

U.S. Bureau of the Census. *The Hispanic Population of the United States: March 1991.* Current Population Reports, Series P-20, No. 455. Washington, D.C.: U.S. Government Printing Office, 1991.

Villafañe, Eldin. *The Liberating Spirit: Toward An Hispanic American Pentecostal Social Ethic.* New York: University Press of America, 1992.

Wagner, C. Peter. *Church Planting for a Greater Harvest.* Ventura, Calif.: Regal, 1990.

Weyr, Thomas. *Hispanics USA: Breaking the Melting Pot.* New York: Harper & Row, 1988.